The CWP and EMHP Handbook

T0385258

of related interest

Brief Behavioural Activation for Adolescent Depression
A Clinician's Manual and Session-by-Session Guide
Laura Pass and Shirley Reynolds
Illustrated by Masha Pimas
ISBN 978 1 78775 502 4
eISBN 978 1 78775 503 1

Cool Connections with CBT for Groups, 2nd edition
Encouraging Self-Esteem, Resilience and Wellbeing in
Children and Teens Using CBT Approaches
Laurie Seiler
Illustrated by Adam Alan Freeman
ISBN 978 1 78775 247 4
eISBN 978 1 78775 248 1

Video Interaction Guidance
A Relationship-Based Intervention to Promote Attunement, Empathy and Wellbeing
Edited by Hilary Kennedy, Miriam Landor and Liz Todd
ISBN 978 1 84905 180 4
eISBN 978 0 85700 414 7

Creative Ways to Help Children Manage Anxiety
Ideas and Activities for Working Therapeutically with Worried Children and Their Families
Dr. Fiona Zandt and Dr. Suzanne Barrett
Foreword by Dr. Karen Cassiday
Illustrated by Richy K. Chandler
ISBN 978 1 78775 094 4
eISBN 978 1 78775 095 1

Improving the Psychological Wellbeing of Children and Young People
Effective Prevention and Early Intervention Across Health, Education and Social Care
Edited by Julia Faulconbridge, Katie Hunt and Amanda Laffan
Foreword by Sarah Brennan
ISBN 978 1 78592 219 0
eISBN 978 1 78450 496 0

The Mentally Healthy Schools Workbook
Practical Tips, Ideas, Action Plans and Worksheets for Making Meaningful Change
Pooky Knightsmith
Foreword by Norman Lamb
ISBN 978 1 78775 148 4
eISBN 978 1 78775 149 1

The CWP and EMHP Handbook

CBT Essentials with Children and Young People

Hugh Miller

Illustrated by Steve Ham
Foreword by Peter Fonagy OBE

Jessica Kingsley Publishers
London and Philadelphia

First published in Great Britain in 2022 by Jessica Kingsley Publishers
An imprint of Hodder & Stoughton Ltd
An Hachette Company

5

A CIP catalogue record for this title is available from the
British Library and the Library of Congress

ISBN 978 1 83997 151 8
eISBN 978 1 83997 152 5

Printed and bound by CPI Group (UK) Ltd, Croydon CR0 4YY

Jessica Kingsley Publishers' policy is to use papers that are natural,
renewable and recyclable products and made from wood grown in
sustainable forests. The logging and manufacturing processes are expected
to conform to the environmental regulations of the country of origin.

Jessica Kingsley Publishers
Carmelite House
50 Victoria Embankment
London, EC4Y 0DZ, UK

www.jkp.com

Contents

PART 3: TIPS FOR INTERVENTIONS

Foreword

The NHS's 'Long Term Plan' has created the most ambitious vision for mental health provision that the UK has ever seen. It marked the cumulative achievements of several decades of campaigning, research and the implementation of new models of care in placing mental health alongside cardiovascular disease and cancer as the primary objective of our healthcare systems.

Nowhere was this change of priorities more dramatic than in relation to children and young people's mental health. Epidemiological studies have revealed that problems in adult mental health emerge, for the most part, before the age of 25 and in almost half of cases before the age of 14 (Solmi *et al.*, 2021). Early intervention should serve a preventive purpose.

We are working to a plan that will enable one hundred per cent of children and young people with diagnosable mental health problems to receive treatment and care from the NHS within ten years of the plan's launch. This ambition could not be achieved without a radical change in the way the healthcare professions reimagined themselves, and the trainings that they offer. New professions are required if the treatment gap is to be bridged. Implementing the long-term plan for children's mental health demands a new army of mental health professionals who are able to provide effective evidence-based interventions, following relatively brief trainings, but working in a system that supports them to ensure safe practice. Children's Wellbeing Practitioners (CWPs) and Education Mental Health Practitioners (EMHPs) are examples of the new psychological professions that will ensure that the ambitious goals that we have for addressing the mental health needs of our children and young people are met.

The key is education and training. There is no shortage of people wanting to enter these professions, but they need training to equip them to rapidly master the complex challenges which mental health problems present. This is a much-needed book to empower those wanting to enter psychological professions to do so in a confident and productive way. The author and contributors are to be congratulated for providing a useful tool to help us in our ambitious journey to create a world where all children and families are supported to effectively build on their strength and achieve their full potential.

Professor Peter Fonagy OBE
Chief Executive, Anna Freud National Centre for Children and Families and National Clinical Advisor on Children's Mental Health, NHS England

Contributors and Acknowledgements

Thanks to all my current and former colleagues at Brighton's Schools Wellbeing Service, Brighton Specialist CAMHS and the Anna Freud Centre, and the many practitioners and teachers in the wider psychology world who've contributed to this book. It really is such a generous, supportive community.

I'd particularly like to thank the following. To let them off the hook, I should point out that none of the following practitioners and trainers are endorsing the book's content – they have just helpfully contributed to various chapters.

Julia Avnon is a clinical psychologist and a clinical tutor at the Anna Freud Centre and kindly contributed ideas to Chapter 15 on 'back-up teams'.

Cara Bean got across some of the many experiences of having anxiety in a way that just isn't possible in words.

Octavia Bell and Emily Blake lead a duty and risk team within a Specialist CAMHS service, and kindly contributed their thoughts on effective safety planning and risk assessment. They're also the best CAMHS colleagues you could ask for during a lockdown.

Paige Clarke is a CWP tutor at the Anna Freud Centre and helped review chapters in the first section of this book.

Vicki Curry is my hero. She's the co-author of *CBT with Children, Young People and Families* (2012) and the director of the CBT and CWP programmes at the Anna Freud Centre. When teaching, Vicki's passion for this stuff just beams out of her. I was very lucky to do my CBT training under Vicki's watchful eye, even more lucky to end up working in her CWP tutor team, and triple-y lucky to have Vicki's support for this project. Vicki generously reviewed and contributed heavily to the anxiety chapters.

Kirsty Drysdale is a qualified Children's and Young People's Wellbeing Practitioner and a specialist lecturer on the CYWP course at the Greater Manchester Psychological Therapies Training Centre. Kirsty kindly reviewed and contributed to Chapters 1 and 6.

Suzanne Everill contributed ideas to the 'What to Do When Things Get Stuck' chapter. Suzanne is an EMHP at Herefordshire and Worcestershire Health and Care NHS Trust.

Peter Garwood is a senior lecturer in CBT at the University of Sussex. Peter kindly gave permission for a couple of anecdotes from his training, even though he now thinks everyone will think him an ogre – which he isn't. I don't think.

Zoe Goode is a CBT therapist and parenting practitioner with several years' experience in schools. Zoe kindly helped review lots of chapters and made two excellent book title suggestions that didn't quite make the cut in the end – including 'wellbeing knowledge for working in a college' and 'frontline tools for fools in schools'.

Isabel Gregory is an educational psychologist and an honorary lecturer on UCL's EMHP postgraduate diploma programme. As a co-tutor, she was the best partner in crime I could ever hope for. Isabel's excellent facilitation skills helped elicit several of the best ideas from trainee and qualified EMHPs in this book.

Steve Ham fired out the illustrations at such a rapid rate I couldn't write fast enough.

Lauren Hassan-Leslie and Kimberley Saddler kindly helped review and contribute to the 'Ten Ways to Be a More Inclusive Practitioner' chapter. Lauren and Kimberley are tutors on the CWP course team at the Anna Freud Centre.

Jo Lamprinopoulou contributed ideas to lots of chapters – thanks Jo! She's a clinical tutor at the Anna Freud Centre, a psychodynamic and CBT psychotherapist, and a locality lead in a CAMHS service.

Stuart Landsell is a CWP clinical tutor at the Anna Freud Centre and a supervisor. Stuart helped with ideas on structuring sessions and key skills in assessment, with valuable input into inclusive practice.

Maria Loades is a senior lecturer in Clinical Psychology at Bath University and a renowned adolescent mental health researcher. Maria made several helpful corrections and updates to the book.

Gavin Lockhart is the founder of the low intensity postgraduate trainings at the University of Sussex and the clinical lead for CYP mental health at NHS England South East – he put me right on the difference between following protocols and manuals!

Sally McGuire is a kick-ass clinical psychologist and generously reviewed the entire first manuscript, made lots of suggestions and sorted out the formatting into the 'tell them what you'll show them, show them, then tell them what you've shown them' format. Thanks Sally.

Andia Papadopoulou is a clinical psychologist and a clinical tutor at the Anna Freud Centre, and the joint manager of Islington's early years service. She is the co-editor and co-author of *Collaborative Consultation in Mental Health: Guidelines for the New Consultant* (2017). Andia's help with the first two chapters is greatly appreciated.

Shirley Reynolds is an expert on the research and treatment of adolescent depression. She's currently Professor of Evidence Based Psychological Therapies at the University of Reading. Shirley kindly cast her expert eye over Chapter 17 and other sections, and made me promise to never be too dismissive of purely cognitive approaches.

Sam Thompson is a mental health nurse, CAMHS CBT therapist and an EMHP supervisor in Wiltshire. Sam helped review chapters and contributed ideas on effective assessment and good therapeutic conversations.

David Trickey reviewed the section on traumatic bereavements and added lots of insights. David is a clinical psychologist, trainer, co-director of the Trauma Council and a consultant specialising in trauma treatments.

Jaki Watkins is a highly experienced interpersonal psychotherapist and counsellor with over a decade of experience embedded in schools and community settings. Jaki gave lots of valuable contributions to Chapter 24: Working Within Schools.

Lastly, thanks to the whole CYP-IAPT course team at King's College London for creating their excellent manuals and making them freely available for everyone's use. A lot of the thinking behind these manuals has informed the content of this book.

Introduction

THE AIM OF THIS BOOK

A very warm welcome, and thanks for picking up this book! I really hope it's helpful in what can be a highly demanding role. As an Education Mental Health Practitioner (EMHP) or Children's Wellbeing Practitioner (CWP), you have to think on your feet, manage a caseload, deal with emotional distress and try not to get indigestion as you cram down a sandwich on the way to your next session.

Having worked in schools for ten years, I've got some understanding of how challenging the work can be. That's where the idea for this book took shape – in the difficult, awkward moments, the sessions that haven't gone well, the times when I've thought *'I haven't got a clue what to say next.'* Along the way, I've been lucky enough to learn from some amazing colleagues, and this book is crammed with loads of great tips, scripts and tools from EMHPs and CWPs, tutors and lecturers, Child and Adolescent Mental Health Services (CAMHS) practitioners and school practitioners. If you too feel you've sometimes been thrown in at the deep end, then hopefully some of the ideas inside this book will act as a kind of survival jacket to help keep you floating above the waterline – no, scratch that – powering your way through to the finish line like an Olympic swimmer.

ABOUT THE ROLES

If you're reading this you might be training to be an EMHP or CWP. Equally, you might be a counsellor or therapist interested in developing your knowledge and abilities in evidence-based practice. Both the EMHP and CWP trainings are year-long courses that teach core skills in mental health work – the EMHP programmes are a bit more packed, as they include extra modules to prepare students for working specifically in schools. So, while the CWP courses are generally postgraduate certificates, the EMHP courses are postgraduate diplomas. CWPs are usually linked in with CAMHS and third sector mental health services, while EMHPs work within Mental Health Support Teams, which are commissioned to work in schools. The training for both roles is full time and is a mix of university teaching and tutor groups and 'on-the-job' experience with your employer.

THE BOOK'S STRUCTURE

The book is split into three sections: setting yourself up to succeed, practice essentials and tips for interventions.

The first section covers the basics of low intensity cognitive behavioural approaches and why we use them as the basis for our work in early interventions. It also looks at the important practicalities around how to introduce yourself, manage demands, look after yourself and work with parents and carers – often a daunting prospect for new trainees.

'Practice essentials' expands on some really important aspects of our work. It looks at key skills in assessment, goal setting and structuring each session. We identify practical ways to work more openly and effectively with identity and difference. We look at how we can keep safeguarding and risk at the forefront of our minds, and how we can best talk with young people when working together to keep them safe. There's a particular focus on generating good therapeutic conversations with young people, and some ideas around using creativity to improve access and engagement. It also includes advice on self-reflective practice and making the most of supervision.

'Tips for interventions' homes in on what can help when we're in the thick of our work helping young people and families with low mood and anxiety. We concentrate on the importance of psychoeducation for these difficulties and also the all-important cogs that surround the work, such as back-up teams, coping skills and relaxation activities, sleep issues and problem-solving skills. This section also covers how we can best help an intervention 'stick' with good relapse prevention planning and what to do when the sessions don't seem to be helping. The EMHP and CWP trainings teach students comprehensive intervention-specific instruction: think of these tips for interventions as being like a few nice biscuits on the side of the cappuccino served to you by your university lecturers.

Last, we look at some specifics around working in schools including 'whole school approaches', running school staff consultations and taking part in triage meetings, working with school avoidance and school exclusions, how to set up groups and workshops and some thoughts on helping with traumatic incidents.

Throughout the book some advanced skills are distinguished from the main text – these are suggestions for qualified and experienced practitioners wanting to further their practice in partnership with their supervisors. All sections marked with a ✶ can be downloaded for your personal use from www.jkp.com/catalogue/book/9781839971518

WHAT THIS BOOK ISN'T

This isn't a comprehensive low intensity interventions manual. Different trainings teach different approaches, and the hope is that this book coalesces around mental health practice in secondary schools. The book doesn't delve into direct one-to-one work with younger primary school-aged children, and nor does it cover parent-led interventions for challenging behaviour. Indeed, if you're completely new to behavioural activation, graded exposure, parent-led cognitive behavioural therapy (CBT) or parenting programmes such as the Webster-Stratton or Triple-P models then getting training in these, having appropriate supervision, and buying the recommended books and manuals will be essential before you start any practice. This is more of a 'field guide' for practitioners – it assumes a level of training and experience is already in place.

Mixing clinical skills in the education and community settings is no easy task, and I can't stress how challenging mental health work in these frontline positions can be. So – good on you for getting involved in this fantastic work. There's no start or end point in mental health work – it's a continuous journey of learning – and I hope some of the ideas in this book help you thrive in your role. You deserve to!

Part 1

SETTING YOURSELF UP TO SUCCEED

CHAPTER 1

Low Intensity CBT

What You Really Need to Know

'Hey babes, how was your day?'

'Yeah, it was great, I used some behavioural activation principles to engage in an alternative activity – going to the park – and afterwards I rated my ACEs really highly! I really think I'm cracking the maintenance cycle that was fuelling my low mood and I'm feeling better for it.'

'Er, okay…'

Psychology and CBT language is plain weird. In this section we'll look at some of the key concepts behind the work we do to help children and young people, explaining some of the jargon and making it all as accessible as possible.

THIS CHAPTER COVERS:

- How CBT is a range of different therapies that all follow similar principles
- The differences between CBT and non-directive therapies
- What guided self-help is
- The basics of formulating and understanding maintenance factors
- Why changing what we do is particularly useful for helping young people with anxiety or depression

- The advantages of evidence-based practice
- The pros and cons of using manuals for interventions
- How routine outcome measures can help

CBT: IT'S BIGGER THAN YOU MIGHT THINK

CBT tends to way undersell itself. Having trained first as an integrative child psychotherapist and later as a CBT therapist, I've been amazed at the number of different interventions contained within CBT. When starting my CBT training, I felt like I was walking into a supermarket expecting to buy a pint of milk and some bread. Two years later it was like I'd emerged pushing a huge trolley load of food from every section imaginable.

'CBT encompasses a range of talking therapies,' as comedian and former mental health nurse Jo Brand says in her 60-second explainer video on YouTube[1] (it's a great resource to quickly explain what CBT is to a client, by the way). And within the range of different cognitive behavioural therapies are lots of different models and approaches, each developed for specific difficulties – whether that's social anxiety, post-traumatic stress disorder (PTSD), obsessive compulsive disorder (OCD) or phobias.

These models were originally developed for adults but over the years they've been adapted for children and young people taking into account their differing cognitive abilities and other factors. As such, the way we'd look to help a 14-year-old with low mood is very different from what we'd use to help an adult with PTSD, or an eight-year-old with OCD. Even within the umbrella of anxiety presentations, there's a big range of different CBT models for different kinds of anxiety – whether that's generalised anxiety, social anxiety, specific phobias or panic.

What binds different CBT approaches together is the understanding that thoughts, feelings and behaviours are all linked. CBT approaches are also glued together by common principles including the importance of scientific research and development as well as the need to set up sessions properly and encourage clients to try new

---

1   www.youtube.com/watch?v=ZRijYOJp5e0

things out between sessions. What I find really exciting about CBT is it never stands still. It's an endless upward drive of research and improvement, and the learning never stops. 'We're never finished', as clinical psychologists Laura Pass and Shirley Reynolds put it (2020).

COUNSELLING AND CBT

'If it works, it's CBT,' a person-centred counsellor once told me, a wry smile on his face. His comment revealed some of the friction between different therapeutic orientations, and perhaps a little resentment among some counsellors around the emerging predominance of CBT. It's understandable – and there's also some truth in the comment. CBT researchers actively look for what works and a whole gamut of approaches get borrowed and integrated. However, while CBT perches on the shoulders of giants (and integrates ideas from psychodynamic, Gestalt, systemic and other models) it is far from fully effective, and there's a huge amount of work to do to keep improving it.

Many counselling approaches focus on the therapeutic relationship to effect change, putting listening, empathy and encouragement at the heart of practice. In National Institute for Health and Care Excellence (NICE) guidance, counselling is referred to as 'non-directive supportive therapy' (NDST). In CBT the therapeutic relationship is also crucial, and practitioners track their skills in providing a good therapeutic relationship through competency scoring. While focusing on these core skills, therapists then mix in the 'active ingredients' that have been shown to help others facing similar difficulties. When done well, it's a meeting of two minds where the therapist helps their client find their own solutions while offering a protocol and framework they've been trained to deliver.

Like any therapy, CBT can be done poorly – for example, if it's too directive, or the client doesn't feel listened to. I've been guilty of this at times. Having an intervention model in mind can provoke an overly directive style if we're not careful. Client-centred practice has to be our top priority. For example, a practitioner coming up with a list of home tasks for their client to do and then instructing them to do them is a classic example of poor practice. It should be the client thinking they want to change, that it's a good idea to try new things, and to plan how to most effectively give them a go – our job is to facilitate this process with encouragement, support and evidence-based practice know-how. In my own experience, clients often don't complete between-session tasks if they don't feel like it's their idea, or they don't understand the reason behind the tasks or why they might be helpful. This is covered in Chapter 23.

GUIDED SELF-HELP AND LOW INTENSITY WORK

'Guided self-help' and 'cognitive behavioural interventions' are types of 'low intensity work' and are ways of describing what CWPs and EMHPs offer which is distinct from what 'high intensity' cognitive behavioural therapists deliver. What's the difference between low and high intensity work I hear you ask? Well, sometimes it's very blurred – we all work in a very similar way, offering specific interventions for specific problems, with the focus being on the young person helping themselves, and learning new life skills, with the practitioner's help. One distinguisher is that in low intensity practice we're generally pegged to offering around eight sessions. High intensity CBT therapists might offer 10–25 sessions. Another distinguisher is that the additional training high intensity therapists receive means they can work with a broader range of presentations and increased complexity (including risk). In this book I use 'CBT' and 'cognitive behavioural interventions' somewhat interchangeably. I have no idea who came up with the terms 'high intensity' and 'low intensity' and they seem a little unfair: there's nothing low intensity about seeing several young people a week in a hectic school environment!

'FORMULATION': MAKING SENSE OF THINGS

Early on with our clients we work hard with them to make sense of their difficulties. Through our assessments we try to identify what's going on and what intervention might work best. As part of this work we might draw out timelines to identify when the problem started or got worse, and also diagrams to think about a difficult experience in terms of what they thought, how they felt and what they did.

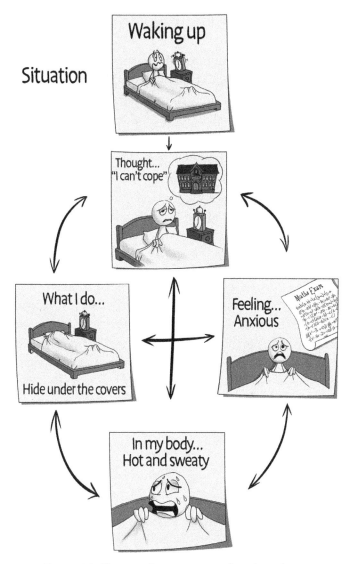

Figure 1.1: Using sticky notes can make a formulation more flexible and collaborative

Once that's done we start to draw out a diagrammatic picture of what's happening for our client – either on paper, on a whiteboard or through screen sharing if working online. This is called a 'CBT formulation' or a 'five aspects formulation' – the five aspects being the situation, thoughts, emotions, body sensations and behaviours (see Figure 1.1). In low intensity work we often boil it down to three aspects: thoughts, feelings and behaviours – with feelings incorporating both emotions and body sensations.

Thinking about experiences in this way might be very new to young people. It's usually helpful to bring in a couple of examples to help demonstrate how feelings, thoughts and behaviours link up.

One idea could be to ask: 'You hear a loud bang at night. What do you think? What do you feel? And what do you do next?' We can then separate our client's thoughts, feelings and actions on a piece of paper or by using sticky notes, as in Figure 1.2. A young person might describe feeling scared, thinking someone might have kicked a door in, and reaching for a baseball bat. Or they might think – has someone fallen over? And, feeling worried, run down the stairs to help. There could be all manner of different responses. The point is, we all react differently to events. To help open this out, we could say:

> 'Now imagine it's bonfire night in November. One person lives in the UK and knows about the firework celebrations that happen every year, whereas another person is American, is visiting the UK for the first time and has never heard of the 5th of November traditions before. How might each of them respond differently to a loud bang?'

We could then draw out another two diagrams, showing how the two people's experiences differ.

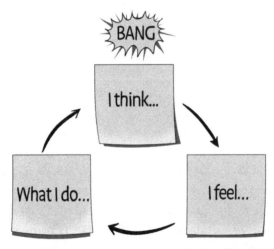

Figure 1.2: Use an everyday situation to explore how feelings, thoughts and what we do can all link up and affect each other

Another idea could be to talk about someone forgetting to bring in their homework, and thinking *'I've done it again, I'm so stupid.'* Another person might think *'No wonder I forgot, I've got a lot on at the moment.'* How would each of them feel differently, and what might they do next?

These examples help a young person become familiar with the idea that how we think affects how we feel and act – and equally, how we feel affects how we think and act, and of course, what we do also affects what we think and how we feel.

When looking at a young person's difficulties a formulation is best done as a joint exercise with the young person, with them writing things down on sticky notes and arranging them on a sheet of paper. This encourages a more client-led approach. We can encourage the young person to draw arrows between the different aspects of their experience, so they can think it through themselves and pull it all together. If a practitioner does all the work, it robs the client of their sense of ownership of the experience and formulation. If working online, we can share screens and move text boxes and arrows around, following the client's guidance.

By the way – a five aspects formulation shouldn't be confused with a 'five Ps formulation', which is another kind of formulation. A 'five Ps' is most commonly used in risk assessment (see Chapter 11). Some universities do also teach trainees to use it for problem-focused assessments, but we look at a different, more user-friendly model for this in Chapter 6.

'MAINTENANCE FACTORS': THE STUFF THAT KEEPS THE DIFFICULTY GOING

In low intensity work, we move from looking at how thoughts, feelings and behaviours connect and interact with each other to cause anxiety or low mood to then exploring a simple model of how these connections keep the problem going. The aim of this exploration is to help our clients understand how they might be staying depressed or anxious – in other words, what is 'maintaining' their difficulties.

The idea is that if we can help them identify what's keeping the difficulty going, we can then help them experiment with changing it (whether that is changing how they think or what they do) and see if it makes them feel better.

For example – if our client is scared of taking a maths test or being asked questions in maths class, they might be tempted to fake being ill and avoid going in to class. By avoiding the situation, they 'stay safe' in the short term, but it'll mean they'll continue to feel anxious about going into maths next week. Their avoidance keeps the anxiety going.

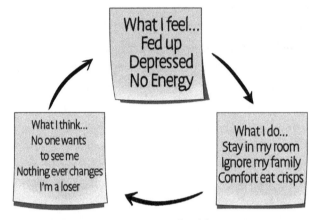

Figure 1.3: A vicious cycle of depression

Equally, if a young person is feeling down, lacking energy and can't be bothered to see their friends, they might feel a bit better just staying at home for the afternoon and cancelling plans. However, if they keep avoiding their friends and end up staying in their room every weekend eating rubbish and bingeing on social media, they'll likely get used to doing very little, continue to feel unmotivated and in the long run risk feeling even worse. Figure 1.3 shows how a vicious cycle of depression can develop. They'll never get that buzz and lift they used to enjoy when seeing their friends. They might eventually start to doubt if their friends even want to see them given how many times they've cancelled. The low mood is likely to keep going unless they break the cycle. There's much more on this in the intervention chapters later in this book.

So – 'maintenance factors' is simply a fancy term that describes the things that keep the problem going. In both cases, it may be that our clients' actions help them feel better in the short term, but in the long term their actions actually make things worse, and they never get to overcome the problem.

While we practitioners might grasp this concept quite quickly, it's quite a weird concept for anyone to wrap their head around. If we don't spend enough time exploring a young person's experience and unearthing likely maintenance factors then there's not much point going any further. It's a bit like digging in a garden and getting all the weeds out – we need to spend time digging out the roots. There's no point just planting new flowers without doing that first.

Another useful analogy is to think about going on a hiking trip. When we set out we need a map to understand the terrain and plot a route. Drawing out a formulation that includes maintenance factors is like getting out a blank sheet of paper and starting to create a map. It's essential we have a solid idea of what's around us before we can take the first steps on the journey.

The formulation should also dictate what intervention we're going to offer – there should be a clear link.

'It sounds obvious, but it's something I find myself reminding students regularly... it all needs to work together!' CWP lecturer Kirsty Drysdale advises.

And just as we'd pull out our map or load it up on our phone to check directions every now and again on our journey, we do the same with the formulation to check it's still right, or to update it or alter our route.

TRY IT OUT: a difficult situation

Ask a friend or family member to describe a recent difficult situation where they felt a difficult emotion. Identify the trigger or situation first, and then try to separate out thoughts, emotions and actions. It's a big ask for people who've never thought about the difference between thoughts and emotions – you could experiment with using lists of common thoughts, emotions and actions to make this easier.

WHY THE FOCUS ON WHAT WE DO?

Some low intensity trainings concentrate on teaching cognitive change methods while others focus more on changing behaviour. Both are of course valid ways of improving wellbeing – there's tons of CBT research to back that up. But within this book (and down to my experience working at the Anna Freud Centre) we're going to talk more about behaviour change. It's a big 'B' and a little 'c' in our low intensity CBT. Let me explain why.

When the main vehicle for change is through doing things differently the hope is that this will help our client start to feel better and start to think differently too. Our client won't need to spend weeks and weeks writing out thought records if they can instead learn to tolerate their anxiety and get into those situations they find difficult. While it'll be challenging, eventually our client will start to think of themselves as more capable – and confidence will slowly replace anxiety.

As mentioned before, child and adolescent CBT approaches have been developed from adult CBT models which tend to incorporate lots of cognitive change methods. However, the evidence that's now emerging is that behavioural approaches might be even better than cognitive approaches (Brett *et al.*, 2020).

And recent advances in scientific understanding have revealed just how different child and teen brains are from those of adults. Professor Shirley Reynolds (Pass and Reynolds, 2020) reminds us that adolescents are still in the fullest flushes of development, though we practitioners so often overlook this fact. One key aspect to consider is that the teen brain's 'executive functioning' is still woefully undeveloped. That means things like planning, problem solving, paying attention and thinking flexibly aren't as easy for teens as they are for adults. 'Thinking about thinking' is especially hard – which won't come as a surprise to any parent!

And with teenage depression, we know the brain's working memory – the equivalent of a computer's RAM – gets clobbered (Fisk, Ellis and Reynolds, 2019), making it harder to recall and remember stuff. If a young person can't think straight because they're depressed, then asking them to think about their thoughts might not work that well. As Shirley Reynolds says, it's a bit like asking someone with a broken leg to just put more weight on the broken leg!

INVOLVING PARENTS

We try to involve parents and carers in the work for a number of reasons – here are three quick ones.

First, teenagers are part of a system. If they live in a family, then their parents will be in a position to help support them in their efforts to improve their wellbeing. This extra support can be particularly helpful given what we know about the adolescent brain – more on this in Chapter 15.

Second, younger children are hugely influenced by their parents. While a practitioner might spend 45 minutes with a ten-year-old, a parent will be with them up to 168 hours a week – so it's a good idea to involve the whole system in helping a younger child. Indeed, when working with primary-school aged children, some approaches advocate working solely with the parents to make changes.

Third – and this is covered in much more depth later in the book – parents have the primary responsibility for looking after their young children and teenagers. Practitioners need to learn to work sensitively and thoughtfully with parents to ensure kids are kept safe. Sadly, we know that kids struggling with mental health difficulties are more likely to hurt themselves or have thoughts around wanting to die. Just as village elders in tribes work together, we have to join with other adults to look after the children and young people in our care.

EVIDENCE-BASED PRACTICE (EBP)

I know the exact moment I realised I needed to train in evidence-based practice. I'd just started a new job working in a new CAMHS in-schools project, and I was doing an assessment with a teenager. The poor girl was visibly anxious as we started the session. We worked through a questionnaire together to find out more about how anxiety was affecting her, and with every box she ticked, I felt more overwhelmed by the scale of her difficulty. I also felt increasingly impotent. Despite my training to date, I'd never been taught a step-by-step approach for helping someone with such debilitating levels of anxiety. To be effective and helpful I knew I needed to sign up for training in evidenced-based approaches designed for specific problems.

But what does EBP actually mean? It's a clunky term and roughly translated it means 'well-trained practitioners delivering interventions that have been shown to work after lots of research'.

A common misconception is that EBP is just a cookbook of techniques where the practitioner blindly follows a manualised approach, disregarding the individuality of the client in front of them for the sake of strict adherence to the treatment protocol they're delivering. And that doesn't sound that great at all.

But at the heart of EBP lies the recognition that clinical expertise is essential for successful treatment. Practitioners have to be really skilled and flexible to ensure good delivery (APA, Presidential Task Force on Evidence-Based Practice, 2006). Strong science underpins both the approaches taught on EMHP and CWP trainings *and* the core skills that practitioners learn to master.

Understandably, EBP was an integral part of the UK government's Green Paper (DoH/DfE, 2017) on transforming children's mental health – the 'design brief' that is shaping the future of Mental Health Support Teams (MHSTs) and other support initiatives.

Of course, there's an array of different therapeutic approaches when helping children with emotional difficulties. However, within a cash-strapped public health service, it's only ethical we focus on interventions proven to work best with specific difficulties.

After several years in CAMHS services, Kirsty retrained as a CWP. She reflects that 'training in evidence-based practice helped me to feel much more equipped as a practitioner.' Kirsty continues, 'it gave me the confidence to know that the support I was offering children and young people was the most likely to be helpful and make a difference.'

NICE RECOMMENDATIONS

In the UK, the National Institute for Health and Care Excellence (NICE) gives the recommendations on what works best for whom. Current NICE guidance is that for all kinds of anxiety, cognitive behavioural interventions should be tried first. For low mood, the evidence isn't quite so strong for CBT, but it is still one of the top recommendations. Although not specifically listed by NICE, the evidence base shows parent coaching works best for behavioural difficulties in primary-school aged children.

HOW CWPS AND EMHPS FIT IN

It's important to adopt a holistic approach to improving the wellbeing of children and young people. CWPs and EMHPs are just two pieces of the puzzle.

Many schools and services employ excellent counsellors who offer highly valuable interventions. Until fairly recently, government guidance was that schools should use counsellors for a wide range of wellbeing difficulties (DoE, 2016), whereas the evidence base now allows us to be more precise about who should be offered what. Hopefully with good collaboration between different services even more young people can receive appropriate help from the variety of services on offer, including CWPs and EMHPs.

So where do low intensity practitioners fit into the picture? Well, while a plumber is trained in fixing heating systems and boilers, a low intensity practitioner's core skills are in helping with low mood, anxiety and challenging behaviour. And just as you wouldn't call a plumber to fix an electrical socket, an EMHP or CWP probably shouldn't be asked to help a child struggling with friendship difficulties or the bereavement of their nan. A school counsellor might be better placed to help with such difficulties. Equally, if a teacher is concerned that a pupil is developing an eating disorder, then getting some advice from a Specialist CAMHS service or an eating disorder service would be the right move. Chapter 24 looks at the importance of 'triaging' – the process by which the varying different services get referred to the young people they're best placed to help.

INNOVATIONS AND LIMITATIONS

In mental health there's often lots of buzz about new and exciting interventions. Sorry to put a downer on things, but while keeping the importance of evidence-based practice in mind, we have to recognise that many are brimming with 'enthusiasm that is ahead of the evidence' as Farias and Wikholm put it (2016).

At the time of writing, there's lots of enthusiasm for mindfulness-based interventions (MBIs), but a recent meta study has concluded that MBIs produce 'no beneficial effect in anxiety reduction' (Odgers *et al.*, 2020). The researchers state that there is 'no evidence to support investment in school-based mindfulness-based interventions.' Ouch!

Personally, I'm a bit gutted about that as I've come to appreciate the value of mindfulness practice (while being the world's least mindful person – just ask my husband). But perhaps more evidence will emerge down the line. That's what's so fascinating about the whole field of mental health research and provision – it's constantly evolving. As a low intensity practitioner, you'll likely experience many additions and revisions to the manuals and protocols you're taught as the wheels of research continue to roll on.

Last, while we need to be encouraging and to model hopefulness, it's important to be honest about the limitations of *any* kind of therapy. It doesn't work for everyone. The conversation about this with a client needs to be pitched carefully and should explain the factors that help make low intensity CBT more successful (for example, completing home practice tasks).

USING MANUALS – OR NOT!

Let's be honest, session-by-session manuals are a bit marmite: I've grown to love them while I know plenty who hate them with a vengeance.

At some universities, trainees are taught how to use key intervention manuals. These have been developed – and are still in development – marrying what the evidence tells us works with tweaks to make them useful and practical in today's schools and community settings. They aim to help us keep true to the principles that make the approaches effective.

Of course, it's common for trainees and supervisors to feel hemmed in or dragged down by a manualised approach. But learning to work effectively with children, in an engaging, child-centred way, *and* cover the principles of CBT is a huge ask in itself.

Vicki Curry is the CWP director at the Anna Freud Centre. She explained to me that in early CWP cohorts, trainees asked about different approaches, and tutors responded by teaching lots of different techniques.

'What we found is this ended up in both trainees and supervisors being confused as to what to do when,' Vicky says. 'As a result, the effectiveness of the interventions suffered. So, we encourage fidelity to the manuals really to help trainees and supervisors as much as anything.'

Clinical tutor Andia Papadopoulou agrees. 'As a supervisor the manuals help me focus supervision on the parts of an intervention that are within the therapeutic competences and abilities of a trainee,' she says. 'The manuals help me help them do the best work they can with their young clients.'

It's a bit like learning a new language. It's easier to learn how to ask how to catch the bus to the airport in French using one phrase, rather than three different ones – and you're more likely to remember it when you're next in France, late for your flight, too.

Having said all that, many trainings teach a more individualised approach to delivering low intensity CBT. Gavin Lockhart, founder of Sussex University's low intensity CBT courses, says that understanding treatment protocols can help practitioners be more flexible.

'A treatment protocol usually provides some outline of structure and sequencing, whilst a manual may well be more prescriptive on the content of each session, the resources used, the homework tasks set, and the number of sessions provided,' explains Gavin. 'There are clinical arguments on both sides for the relative merits and limitations of individualised versus manualised approaches. While manuals are a little quicker to learn, I think teaching the treatment protocols gives you more room to manoeuvre, meaning you can tailor sessions a little more easily for each individual client.'

Regardless of the materials we use, Gavin maintains it's essential we stick to the following working principles:

1. Always attend to the therapeutic relationship.

2. Develop an individualised formulation and a shared understanding with the child or young person and their caregivers of what is keeping the problem stuck.

3. Have a solid understanding of the theory and key principles behind your intervention strategy so you can share these with your clients.

'I can't stress enough how important it is for everyone to fully understand the rationale for the strategy – this will help support collaboration, engagement and relapse prevention,' says Gavin. 'When this is in place, it enables practitioners to work in a more flexible way while staying true to the principles of the treatment protocol or manual.'

Whether you use manuals or not, it's a lifetime of learning – if not several!

ROMS: MEASURING HOW IT'S GOING

Routine outcome measures (ROMS) help in three ways:

1. They help the assessing process and help identify the young person's biggest difficulty.

2. They help us track how are clients are doing, week by week.

3. They help us build and maintain a good therapeutic alliance.

At the start and end of the intervention most practitioners go through a comprehensive questionnaire with their client and/or their parent. One example is the Revised Children's Adolescent and Depression Scale (Chorpita *et al.*, 2000) – otherwise known as RCADS – which is standard fare in most services and helps dig into different anxiety presentations, as well as low mood and OCD. Another is the strengths and difficulties questionnaire (SDQ) – often used for younger children with challenging behaviour.

Duncan Law is a clinical psychologist and one of the board directors of the Anna Freud Centre's Child Outcomes Research Consortium (CORC). Duncan Law (2021) advises us to take time to explain why we want a young person or parent to complete such a big form, which can take up to 15 minutes of a session and may feel quite intrusive and personal. Consider saying something like this:

'I'm going to ask you fill out this long questionnaire because it'll give us a really good overview of some of the difficulties you might be experiencing. After you've completed it, we'll review it together and discuss it, and then we can come back to it in following sessions too. Most questionnaires we're asked to complete we just send off and never see again, but this one is really crucial to our work. Also, I want you to know that I am someone who's trained in mental health. I am very comfortable with however you answer any of these questions. I won't judge you at all and I want to support you in being as honest as you can.'

TRY IT OUT: routine outcome measures

Using a similar script to that suggested by Duncan Law (see Law and Wolpert, 2014), ask a friend or family member to complete a full RCADS questionnaire. It can be tempting to rush through this and just ask them to fill it out – practise taking it slowly and ensuring they understand just how useful their answers are to you.

It's really important to take some time to discuss the client's answers and think about them together. The RCADS is a useful doorway to open up discussion. A client will feel better understood if their practitioner picks up on particular answers they've given and asks for more detail. For example, we could ask, 'I notice you've said you often struggle with your sleep – how many hours do you normally get? Do you often feel tired?'

As we then progress through each subsequent session, we can use the shorter symptom-specific RCADS questionnaires or alternatively the Clinical Outcome Rating Scales (CORS) forms (Miller, Duncan and Johnson, 2000) if your service has a license to use them. These take just a few minutes and are best done at the start of the session as part of the check-in process. Again, we can use the answers we're given therapeutically, asking for thoughts around why things have changed and so on. We can then compare scores from week to week, to review progress and work out what might be helping things get better or worse. A good trick is to turn the results page sideways – it makes a nice graph to show progress.

There are two other routine outcome measures that we use. 'Goal-based outcomes' help us track progress towards the client's goals, and 'session rating scales' or 'session feedback questionnaires' are ways of asking our clients for feedback on how the sessions have gone. These are covered in Chapters 6 and 8.

TAKE-AWAYS

▶ CBT is a range of therapies, including low intensity cognitive behavioural interventions for specific difficulties like behavioural activation for low mood, and graded exposure for anxiety.

▶ It's really crucial we keep client-centred practice at the heart of everything we do, just like counsellors do.

▶ The formulation is a way of making sense of the difficulty, and what might keep it going (also known as maintenance factors). It helps us decide which intervention to offer.

▶ Advances in science continue to shape what we offer, and we focus quite a lot on changing 'what we do' in child and adolescent evidence-based practice.

▶ While following NICE guidelines, it's important to remain holistic and respect what other practitioners can bring to the table.

▶ Manuals can help as a kind of 'road map' and keep us on the right track – though they are a bit marmite!

▶ It's important to track how progress is going, using 'routine outcome measures' so that both the practitioner and client know they are on the right road to recovery.

CHAPTER 2

How to Introduce Yourself

Your ID badge might say 'mental health practitioner' or 'wellbeing practitioner' but these are new roles, and many people won't have a clue about who you are or what you do. Having a quick way to introduce yourself and explain your role will be incredibly handy.

THIS CHAPTER COVERS:

- How to describe your role to children, young people, teachers and caregivers
- What language to use with different people and age groups
- Ideas from practitioners on how to introduce yourself

DESCRIBING YOURSELF

In the UK, low intensity practitioner roles are brand-spanking new and will be unfamiliar to most people. Equally, it can be hard to describe what the role involves. Getting really familiar with the EMHP and CWP job descriptions outlined on the NHS jobs website is a good starting point, but it doesn't make much sense unless you are familiar with words and phrases like 'interventions', 'low intensity' and 'mild to moderate' which we can't realistically expect anyone in the real world to understand.

So – ditch the jargon and find yourself a quick, succinct way of describing yourself to teachers, children, parents and fellow mental health workers alike.

First, when describing yourself, it's okay to say you're in training. This is a job where honesty really matters. You don't have to do yourself down, though. Be proud of the experience you bring to the table from previous roles. As tutor Andia Papadopoulou reminds us, there's a rigorous process of selection to become a CWP or EMHP and trainees are equipped with lots of valuable skills and experience already.

Andia advises new practitioners to 'learn to connect with these experiences and relay them in your introductions to other adults'. She says, 'You could say something like, "though I am new to this role and I am still training I have a lot of experience of working with children and young people helping them with their difficulties" – that would work.'

Second, it's a good idea to say that EMHPs and CWPs are adding to the existing workforce and helping to bolster the systems as they are. We want to help colleagues feel supported rather than threatened – a freelance school counsellor might feel a little wobbly about their job security knowing someone else is coming in to do a similar role to them. But they don't need to.

Third, it's helpful if you can give a bit of clarity about who you'll be working with. Your service should specify the client group. For example, many of London's Mental Health Support Teams offer the following interventions for particular client groups, as follows:

- guided self-help with low mood and anxiety for young people aged 11–18

- guided self-help for parents of children aged 5–11 who're exhibiting anxiety or challenging behaviour

- workshops and groups for primary school aged children on emotional resilience and wellbeing

- workshops for teachers, parents and carers offering psychoeducation to help support children and young people.

And finally, definitely mention that you'll be helping children and young people engage with programmes that research shows can be most helpful for particular difficulties, including anxiety, low mood and challenging behaviour.

▓ TRY IT OUT: introducing yourself

With a colleague – or even at your next team meeting (you can choose your own level of exposure!) – say you're playing around with how to introduce yourself to parents who may be unfamiliar with your role, and then try it out. Ensure you're clear about who you are, what you do and what your service offers, and if you're a trainee, what previous experience you bring to the role.

TALKING TO SCHOOL STAFF

If you're in a MHST based out in the wild west of schools then it might take you time to get your head around what can be quite complex organisations.

'Schools can be intimidating environments for a new EMHP,' says Andia.

'You might feel like you've been parachuted into a system with existing practitioners like counsellors and CAMHS practitioners – or you might be all on your lonesome. Exploring your place in things with colleagues will be important.'

Andia also suggests talking with the school's mental health lead about introducing yourself to all the teachers at a staff meeting. You could also print up a card to give out. Ensure school staff know you are coming in from an external agency and won't be contactable through school email systems and so on.

Something like this would work well as an introduction:

'Hi, I'm Jameel, I'm a trainee Educational Mental Health Practitioner from the Barnet Mental Health Support Team. I'm going to be here on Tuesdays, and I'll be assessing and working with young people with emotional wellbeing needs that the special educational needs coordinator (SENCO) and my team agree are appropriate referrals. The whole idea is for my team to add to the current networks of support within schools. We will be using programmes that have been developed through research projects to help with low mood and anxiety.'

TALKING TO CHILDREN AND YOUNG PEOPLE

When it comes to talking with children and young people, well, it might not surprise you to learn that the title 'Education Mental Health Practitioner' was not selected by a focus group of 11-year-olds. It's a particularly weird and difficult title to understand. Not that many job titles make a lot of sense! When I told primary-school children I was a 'school counsellor', most thought that I meant I was on the school council helping Jack in Year 5 and Shanay in Year 6 decide the new playground rules. While teenagers will likely be fine with the EMHP title, consider telling younger kids that you're a 'wellbeing coach' working to help children feel happier.

If you're a CWP then introducing yourself might be slightly easier as you're not so embedded within the school. How about this idea, from clinical tutor Paige Clarke: 'I'm Paige, and I'm a children's wellbeing practitioner, and I help young people who might be having problems like worries or low mood. I'm here to see if you'd like any help and to explain a bit about how we'd work together using a step-by-step approach to make things better for you.'

It's often useful to use analogies to explain your role. For example, you could say, 'a bit like a coach might help you get better at football, I help young people develop skills to help them get on top of their worries.'

Another analogy might be, 'when young people are struggling with low mood, they can sometimes do with a bit of extra help. A bit like having someone come over to help you get your phone or laptop back running at full speed again.'

Practise and see what fits for you. Have a couple of scripts up your sleeve so you can feel more confident in explaining who you are and what your role is. This will help you enormously when it comes to keeping boundaries nice and clear – more on this in the next chapter.

TALKING TO PARENTS AND CARERS

Chapter 5 covers meeting parents and carers in more depth, but do think about how you might explain your role. Paige Clarke suggests the following for parents of teenagers who you might be offering one-to-one support to:

'I'm a Children's Wellbeing Practitioner and I will be working with your child to help them understand their current difficulties with their anxiety or low mood and helping them to find and practise helpful ways to make changes and improve this for them. I may also be checking in with you every now and then as it's really important for parents to be supporting their child's progress outside of sessions so I'm also here to help support you to support your child with that.'

TAKE-AWAYS

► Bear in mind that many school staff, parents and young people won't understand the roles of EMHPs and CWPs, so clarity is crucial.

► Tailor your language to suit the young person's age and ability to understand. Avoid phrases like 'intervention', 'cognitive behavioural psychotherapy', 'low intensity' and 'mild to moderate'.

► Try to make it succinct but use your own natural speaking style so it flows easily.

► Analogies and metaphors can help children and young people of different ages and developmental levels understand your role more easily.

CHAPTER 3

How to Boundary Your Role

If you're reading this it's pretty much a given you're passionate about improving young people's lives. But the very loveliness of what makes you who you are might also make it difficult for you to say 'no' to people. This is a really crucial skill to learn for the sake of your own sanity and also to help make your practice as effective as possible.

> ## THIS CHAPTER COVERS:
>
> - Why it's important to stick within the role
> - How getting pulled in different directions can affect us
> - How to acknowledge, empathise and signpost to other services
> - How to keep communication boundaries
> - Some pointers on good professional practice

You are not Super Therapist™. You can't fix everything. You can't help every child or young person who needs it. And you definitely can't adopt any of them, no matter how sad their stories (just in case you were wondering).

In fact, you will burn yourself out very quickly if you can't learn how to politely decline all manner of requests. And you *can* do this in a kind way – promise.

Saying 'no' can feel blunt and unhelpful, and it can provoke feelings of anxiety around coming across as rude. At worse, we can end up feeling like we're being cold and obstructive. But let's just turn this on its head. Think about it: a practitioner has limited capacity. We need to stay on target, providing interventions we've been trained in that have a solid evidence base, and working only with referrals that have gone through the correct channels. If we start doing work outside of this tight remit, not only is it unclear if it'll be successful or not, but we'll also have less time to offer evidence-based practice to appropriate referrals.

The national target set in the 2017 Transforming Children and Young People's Mental Health Provision green paper (DoH/DfE, 2017) was to reach 35 per cent of all children with mental health needs – a target rightly described as a 'paucity of ambition' by many. So we really need to focus on what matters and help with what we really can help with. Getting your head round this wider context can help bolster your sense that saying 'no' is often the right thing to do.

And the things you might be asked to do might make your head boggle. Educational psychologist Isabel Gregory tells a story where she'd just arrived at a primary school and buzzed herself through the gates. The deputy headteacher rushed out from reception, panting frantically, and asked Isabel if she'd help scrape up the remains of a dead seagull from the playground. 'You've got to help, its nearly break time and the children will be emotionally distraught if they see it!' he pleaded.

So – Isabel dropped her bags and set to it with a shovel and ended up being late in to do her statutory assessment.

I've been asked to cancel booked appointments and instead offer crisis sessions with suicidal teenagers. Facing the pleas of a senior teacher, it took a lot of resolve – and feeling totally heartless – to state that it wasn't within my role and it wouldn't be appropriate.

The more embedded you are in a school or community setting, the more you'll likely become the 'go-to' person for mental health crises – or anything to do with wellbeing. And too much of that is just not healthy for you, or anyone else.

Working online can provoke difficulties with boundaries too. There's obviously a temptation to cut corners – because phones and laptops give us so much flexibility. Maybe a caregiver will be online on their phone while driving their car or with a screaming baby on their laps. I've experienced both – thankfully on separate occasions. It's okay to look out for yourself and them in this kind of a situation, and just say, 'Hey, I need to be able to think in order to be helpful to you... Shall we do this session when you're in a quiet space and able to focus too?'

ACKNOWLEDGE, EXPLAIN AND SIGNPOST

How do we say no politely? Clinical psychologist Vicki Curry suggests following three key steps:

1. Acknowledge the difficulty and empathise.

2. Explain that while you might like to help it's not something you can help with directly as it's not part of your role.

3. Give signposting advice on suitable services.

It's normal to feel stressed and anxious in these situations. It just means you're human and you care! If you're feeling stuck, give yourself some breathing space and say you'll talk with your team or supervisor first, and get back to them. When working on your own this is a really good practice to get into. It reduces that sense of feeling personally responsible for many of the decisions you're asked to take.

KEEPING IN TOUCH

When you're providing any kind of therapeutic service it's good practice to keep solid boundaries. While it might be tempting to give out our phone number or email address to concerned parents and teachers and know it'd be really easy to text someone to change an appointment time, think carefully about this first with your supervisor. This work is emotionally demanding, and you need to contain those demands as best you can within the working day. You are also not a 'crisis line' for the people you work with.

It's also good practice to only share contact details with other professionals. There might be a key contact person at your school or service who you can direct calls and communications to. For appointment reminders your service might set up a generic team email address that all practitioners can share and use. This helps cushion practitioners from out-of-hours calls and emails.

If a parent asks you for your direct number or email address and you feel awkward about saying no, just blame your organisation and say it's against their rules. The NHS trust I work for doesn't allow employees to share their email addresses with caregivers. Sometimes I've been CC'd into messages with a network of professionals and a parent, and the parent has then emailed me directly. On these occasions I've had to ring them to say I can't reply via email due to trust policies. It sounds ridiculous, but by reducing others' expectations on me to respond on my days off it helps protect my own wellbeing.

TRY IT OUT: challenging situations

To learn how to demarcate our roles it's worth practising our responses to many of the demands and requests that might come hurtling our way. Try out the following role plays with a colleague. There are no right or wrong answers – but it's useful to experience what it's like to be put in uncomfortable situations and learn how to pause, take stock, and try to work out how to respond appropriately.

- A parent stops you in the school car park and asks if you can work with his 15-year-old son who's been very down recently.

- A deputy head asks to talk to you about his son, who is feeling really anxious about going to secondary school.

- A teacher bursts into your room and asks you to help talk to a seven-year-old you assessed last week who is highly distressed and trying to leave school right now.

- Your MHST team lead asks you to make a home visit to a 13-year-old whose adult sister has sadly just died.

- A school counsellor asks you for advice on a child who he thinks is developing OCD behaviours.

STICKING WITHIN THE ROLE

On paper the role is nice and tightly defined. In practice, it quickly gets woolly. EMHPs and CWPs are commissioned to help children and young people with 'mild to moderate' mental health difficulties, specifically anxiety and low mood, as well as challenging behaviour. Within this remit, we can offer specific interventions – for example, workshops for young people on exam stress, or a group for parents of anxious children. MHSTs may also be commissioned to do some 'whole school approach' wellbeing support. Around these core activities, you might also be involved in triage meetings and other meetings with fellow professionals supporting a family. Keep coming back to these core activities, and practise spelling out the limits of your job role.

In your first years of practice you shouldn't reasonably be expected to work with a young person who's continuing to self-harm, has life-impairing OCD or signs of PTSD. Helping children deal with bereavement or friendship issues isn't sufficiently within your remit – think about signposting on to a specialist bereavement charity, or the school's pastoral support workers. Equally, I'd argue you shouldn't be running anti-bullying groups, self-esteem groups or other generic interventions – important as they might be.

It's so easy to be pulled out of your remit, but you are trained in specific interventions for specific problems and it's helpful to remind everyone what they are, particularly as mental health is such a grey area. When needed, remind others of the importance of following NICE guidelines. And keep bringing your focus back onto the holy trinity of depression, anxiety and challenging behaviour.

In my role as a tutor, I've been made aware of several situations where schools or services have expectations that are way out of whack with what CWPs and EMHPs are meant to deliver – no doubt partly because many of the projects are so fresh and new. If you're being asked to do things you're not comfortable with, raise them in supervision or in line management meetings.

PROFESSIONAL PRACTICE ONLINE

Try to keep up the same professional standards wherever you're working – whether in a school or community setting or working online, and whether you're seeing clients or attending training. If you're online, these include being in a quiet undisturbed space (not on the motorway) and staying attentive and focused (not vaping or eating your lunch at the same time). Wear your ID card and lanyard, and try to create as professional a background behind you as is possible (e.g. clear the laundry off the bed!). If you have a dodgy connection or need to turn your video feed off, it's good practice to flag this up as a possibility at the start of a session, and problem solve ahead. And if you're in training and not feeling great – whether physically or emotionally – let the course team and your colleagues know.

GETTING AN AGREEMENT IN WRITING

At the start of an intervention a simple written agreement can help get things off on the right foot. This is known in the business as a 'therapeutic contract'. Within the agreement, you can outline how many sessions you're offering, remind your client about the limits of confidentiality and talk through what happens with no-shows. These are the essentials. You could also usefully use the agreement to position yourself as an eager helper and remind your client just how helpful it is in low intensity CBT to 'give things a go' between sessions. It's best to keep the language jargon-free and accessible – watch out for words like 'discharge' creeping into your writing, and avoid them at all costs! See Table 3.1 for an example of a therapeutic contract.

 Table 3.1: A therapeutic contract

Our agreement
• After today, we'll meet twice more to see if CBT might be helpful for you – then we'll decide how many more sessions we'll do.
• I'll do my very best to understand what's troubling you and I'll work as hard as I can to help you make changes. We'll think up goals together, and help you move forward.
• During our sessions, I'll ask you how we're doing as a team. I'd love it if you can tell me when I get things wrong so I can try and do better.

- We know CBT works best when people try things out between sessions. If we come up with a plan together and you think it's a good idea to try it out then it'd be great if you can give it a shot, and let me know how it goes. If we change nothing, nothing changes!

- Your safety comes first. If I'm worried about you, I'll need to talk to my team and maybe also your carers or parents so we can work together as adults to keep you safe.

- Please come to every session. If you can't make it, ring CAMHS the evening before and leave a message for me – thanks!

- Usually if young people miss two or more sessions without warning then we'd not offer more sessions as we'd think now isn't the right time for this kind of work.

- Please do talk to an adult you trust if you're not liking the sessions or you don't feel comfortable telling me so. Honesty is the best policy!

- Our next session is on_____ (*insert day*) at_____
_____ (*insert time*) at_____ (*insert place*) and I'll look forward to seeing you then.

Signed	Signed

TAKE-AWAYS

► Take care of yourself! Learn that it's okay to say 'no' and bracket your role.

► Practise empathising, and signposting, for a variety of requests that aren't appropriate to your role.

► Be aware of being pulled sideways. Keep coming back to the holy trinity – low mood, anxiety and challenging behaviour – and keep NICE guidelines in mind.

► Regardless of setting, maintain the same standards of professional practice.

CHAPTER 4

How to Look After Yourself

This is a tough gig. In a typical day, it'll take a lot of energy and focus to run two effective one-to-one sessions with young people in the morning. Just as you're writing up your notes, someone will ring you. You won't have enough time to finish your sandwich before you're bundling off to a community centre to run a workshop. If you're new to this line of work, you'll need to prioritise your wellbeing – both for your own sake, and the good of the young people and families you work with.

THIS CHAPTER COVERS:

- The importance of self-care

- Tips from practitioners on how to look after ourselves

- Ideas on how to manage things when they're overwhelming

Self-care is so important, not just for your own wellbeing, but also for ongoing effective practice. There are several elements in the job that can lead to fatigue and burn-out.

There are the demands and stress of the role: the variety of activities and demands, the rushing about and the difficulty in separating away from work after a long day.

Then there's the potential for suffering vicarious trauma from listening to the difficulties of others, which can trigger off things in ourselves.

Also, there's the emotional burden we can feel from not being able to help as much as we'd like – whether that's down to a lack of time, or the length of waiting lists, service constraints or something else.

Sometimes we might have to do something like pass on a safe-guarding concern which a young person isn't happy about – or we might feel we want to go the extra mile to keep them safe by checking they're okay at home, but that doesn't fit with our service protocols. These situations provoke a sense of 'moral injury' – a feeling that we've let someone down but had no sense of choice in the matter.

We may also just feel worn out after a long day of listening and validating others and find it hard to notice when we're suffering from compassion fatigue.

It's normal to feel upset or experience difficult feelings during the work we do. Go talk to someone after a difficult session. It's crucial we check in with our supervisors and colleagues regularly about how we're doing. If you're not used to being open in this way, then take baby steps and slowly learn to trust that it's okay to not be okay.

There's also lots we can do to look after ourselves. No doubt you'll already being doing stuff that recharges and renews you after work – whether its yoga, having a bath while watching a boxset, walking the dog, drinking a glass of wine or having a blast on the Xbox. One trainee said it was cleaning her room that recharged her – we're all different. The important thing is to recognise what it is in your life that gives you a lift and makes you smile, and keep doing it, as often they're the first things we forget to do when our batteries are running low.

We can use a bit of behavioural activation to help us with this. Carve out a 20-minute chunk every day for a week to do something you enjoy that recharges you and commit to it.

Changing your life and what you do even for just 20 minutes a day takes planning and commitment – even more so if you have a hectic family, work or social life. Work out an action plan with a friend or fellow trainee, and ask each other how you'll remember to do it, how you'll record it and what you could usefully remind yourself of when you're struggling with motivation. Good luck!

▨ TRY IT OUT: 20 minutes a day

Commit to doing an enjoyable, relaxing or nurturing activity for at least 20 minutes a day for the next week. Report back to a friend or colleague in seven days' time and have them ask you how it went. (By the way, we need to be able to practise what we preach. If we're going to ask young people to take steps to look after themselves, we need to be able to as well!)

TIPS FROM PRACTITIONERS

By the end of the training year most practitioners feel totally frazzled. One group of EMHPs questioned if they'd have applied if they'd known how tough it would be. Here are some of the group's tips on surviving the year.

> I've had to learn to let things go. I've spent hours ruminating about sessions and how they've gone, questioning myself and saying, 'I should I have done this or that.' I now have a list of positive self-talk statements and if I notice myself going down that rabbit hole I practise using them – stuff like 'I've done my best, keep going, tomorrow will be even better than today.' They help.

Figure 4.1: Writing down positive statements can help with our motivation

· ·

I've had to be really strict with myself and never work at weekends! It's been really hard to bracket them off but having two full days off helps me reset and recharge.

· ·

At a particularly low point during the course, with loads of deadlines hanging over me, I did a 'chairwork' exercise with my supervisor where she asked me to imagine the younger me, the one applying for the course, sitting on a chair opposite me. She asked me to describe the values that drove the younger me to apply to be an EMHP. This helped me connect back to what drove me to do this role and why I'm here in the first place. It was also a reminder that I am a kind person, and that I need to give myself a bit more of that kindness when I get frustrated with myself. I wrote down some practical tips that the 'younger me' would encourage me to follow in times of stress, and they help.

· ·

Figure 4.2: 'I visualise a big switch for my working day and turn it off'

I've learnt to look at who's responsible for progress and a good outcome, and question if it's all my responsibility. It's all so systemic. Sometimes I do a responsibility pie, looking at who is involved in the person's progress. I might only be 25 per cent of that. It has to come from the family too. They have to be engaged. I also do a visualisation when my day is done. I visualise a big switch for my working day and turn it off. I then imagine putting my laptop away in a box and say 'bye-bye work!' When working from home I've realised I probably talk too much about work stress with my family, which isn't good. It's much healthier to have a ten-minute chat with a colleague at the end of each day to off-load.

· ·

I always want my young people to make big improvements and it stresses me out when it doesn't happen. My supervisor told me something really helpful. She said our job purpose is to follow the protocols as best we can, rather than ensuring improvement. This really helped, because obviously lots of other stuff happens in kids' lives – family stuff, friendships and even pandemics. We're all nice and of course we want to help. But we need to unhook ourselves from the expectation we can make everyone better. We just need to follow the manuals and the approaches as best we can, tailored to each young person.

· ·

I hate saying no to people...and I hated even bringing this difficulty up...but I just had to talk to my supervisor about it as I wasn't coping with the essays, case studies and clinical work all at once. She helped me work out my priorities, and we agreed the number one priority was for me to pass the course. If I didn't manage that, nothing else would matter anyway! It was awkward talking about it as I don't like others to think I can't cope, but it was really useful.

· ·

During sessions I often start doubting how things are going... I think 'they're bored...this isn't going well...' and so on. I've learnt to look for the evidence and check in more often with my client. For example, I'll ask, 'are you happy to carry on?' I know I've got a negative mental filter, and this helps me rebalance that. I have to work at not over-thinking, just accepting the young person's answers rather than mind-reading them and doubting they're telling the truth...and that helps the sessions flow a lot better for me.

· ·

WELLBEING MIND MAP

If you're ever feeling overwhelmed this is a useful exercise to identify what's going to help you feel better – see Figure 4.3. Grab a sheet of A4 and write at the top what your signs of stress and overwhelm are. Then draw a line down the middle. Write 'what helps' in the middle of the left box, and 'what doesn't help' on the right. Then think through the things you've done today or in the last few days that have helped you feel better and those that haven't. Then make a plan to drop what doesn't work, and increase doing the things that do help.

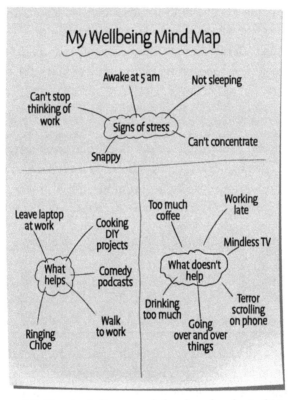

Figure 4.3: If you're feeling overwhelmed, grab a sheet of A4 and draw a mind map thinking through things you've done in the last few days that have helped you feel better, and those that haven't

TAKE-AWAYS

▶ Work out what helps you recharge and deliberately factor it into your working day.

▶ Learn to let things go. At the end of a working day, turn the switch off!

▶ Unhook yourself from big expectations around clients making big improvements.

▶ Use supervision as a sounding board to help you with the stresses and decide priorities.

▶ Self-reflection is great, but watch out for harsh self-criticism and doubt.

CHAPTER 5

Tips When Meeting Parents and Carers

It's good to feel as comfortable and confident as possible when meeting caregivers for the first time. It can feel a little intimidating for new practitioners – but there are some things we can remember and scripts we can use to help us along the way.

THIS CHAPTER COVERS:

- Why we need to really focus on the parents' perspective
- Why a practitioner's age really doesn't matter
- How to answer difficult questions from parents and carers
- Common conundrums when working with parents and carers

THE PARENTS' PERSPECTIVE

Parents and carers come to us having had all kinds of different attitudes towards mental health and schools. Cultural differences may need to be considered as a family might have a very different take on things. It's always worth asking about these, and some ideas are given on how to do this in the chapters that follow. It's also worth noting that many parents still feel a degree of stigma around asking for help for mental health. A recent survey showed that one in three parents would feel other parents would judge them if their children needed wellbeing support (Place2Be, 2021).

In many communities, lots of children go to the same school their parents went to. The parents might have had a fantastic time as children and feel warm and positive coming into school. Alternatively, school might trigger painful memories. Maybe they were bullied, struggled academically or felt unfairly treated by teachers. We just don't know what their experience was like, but whenever parents are asked to meet with teachers and other professionals, it's likely that ripples from the past are going to rise up.

CBT therapist Zoe Goode advises practitioners to really be mindful of these possibilities. This is particularly important if we're planning to help a parent with a child's challenging behaviour because we don't want them to feel criticised or judged in any way.

'Ask a parent where they'd like to meet – it may be that doing it online, or in a neutral place like a café, will feel easier for them', Zoe advises. 'It's also okay to ask them what their own experience of school was like. This can help them separate out their past from the present.' She continues, 'Also, take time to really ask for their perspective on their child. A parent is the expert on their child, and we need to help build their confidence, not make them feel like a failure.'

When working with older teenagers, we'll need to respect the young person's views on involving their parents and carers and be led by them. But it's still really useful to involve parents where possible as part of the young person's 'back-up team', as described in Chapter 15.

PERCEPTIONS AROUND AGE AND EXPERIENCE

Younger trainee practitioners can sometimes feel nervous around working with older parents. This could be down to perceived power and experience imbalances coupled with fears around judgement or 'being seen through'. However, a lot of anecdotal feedback from parents and carers is that they actually prefer a fresh and motivated new practitioner to someone who's been in the game for 30 years. Each year, training universities invite parents and carers who've received help from CWPs and EMHPs to talk about their experiences, and this is a recurring theme. A practitioner's age really isn't a big deal for parents.

Trainees also sometimes worry about telling parents that they're in training. But again, parent feedback consistently affirms a supportive stance towards trainees. Just as most of us wouldn't mind talking to a trainee doctor or physiotherapist, in general parents understand that trainees are at a stage in their training where they're ready to deliver the intervention on offer.

There's also some evidence that fresher practitioners can be as effective as experienced practitioners – including when delivering the parent-led programme for child anxiety developed by Cathy Cresswell and her colleagues (Thirlwall *et al.*, 2013).

As one trainee CWP put it, 'We can remind parents that being a trainee means we've got loads of energy and enthusiasm – we're truly excited to try and help.'

Let's move on to think about some common conundrums.

'ARE YOU A PARENT YOURSELF?'

Perhaps the biggest dilemma for a trainee is how to respond when you're asked if you have children yourself. Now, a parent might ask 'have you got kids?' purely out of interest or curiosity – but then again, it's not something they'd likely ask their bank manager, dentist or plumber. It's a *fairly* safe bet they're asking because you're a mental health professional specialising in helping children and young people – and they want to scope out your level of experience with children or know if you 'get' the challenges of parenting yourself.

However, your parenting status is no metric of your ability to work in this profession. Obviously, plenty of amazing practitioners don't have children themselves.

But how do we deal with this question? We certainly don't have to answer it directly if we don't want to. Here's one possible approach...

Parent: Do you have kids yourself?

Practitioner: Sometimes parents and carers ask me this as they want to check out if I've got enough experience and understanding to work in these often complex areas. Just to reassure you, I have been trained in the best evidence-based approaches for particular difficulties. I approach each child I work with as unique, with no biases. You're the expert in knowing your child and my training is in psychological wellbeing, and the idea is we bring the two together to try to make things better.

If you're ever asked this question, try to avoid falling into that trap of thinking, *'Who am I to offer advice on parenting when I haven't got kids myself?'*

Instead, try thinking, *'Who am I, with my training and passion, to not try to help this parent help their child?'*

It is totally up to you if you tell a parent whether you have children or not. I'd argue that the most appropriate response is to not answer it directly. You are a professional and your personal life doesn't come into it.

OTHER CONUNDRUMS

Here are some other challenging scenarios and ways of responding to them. These situations have all been experienced by practitioners and worked through in supervision. Hopefully they'll give you some food for thought.

Parent: I've actually got my own mental health difficulties. It'd be really good to get some help from you with them.

Practitioner: I'm so sorry to hear that. Thanks for sharing your concerns with me – it sounds like you're going through a tough time. Now I'd love to help, but my role is working with young people and so my focus is on helping them. I'm here in that capacity and I'm not trained to help adults with mental health – but how about we have a look together at some local services that might be helpful for you?

. . . .

Parent: I think this assessment is a waste of time – my child is fine.

Practitioner: I appreciate your perspective. How about if we go back a step – would it be helpful if I go through what my role is first to make that a bit clearer? Perhaps then we could also look through the referral form that the school staff completed outlining the difficulties they are noticing your child is presenting with in school?

. . . .

Parent: No offence, but I think my child needs to be seen by the proper CAMHS service at the hospital.

Practitioner: It sounds like you've got some strong concerns about your child and it'd be helpful for me to hear more about the reasons you think they need help from CAMHS. First though can I tell you a bit more about how our service fits into the picture? We're an early intervention service and we're here to increase access and speed things up. The general guidance is for our service to provide the first level of help and we would then refer up to Specialist CAMHS if needed. But as I say it'd be really helpful to hear your concerns first so we can work together to help your child as best we can in whichever service is most appropriate.

. . . .

Situation: Parents bombard you with information and their personal problems and you feel overwhelmed with their own difficulties and issues.

Practitioner: I'm sorry to interrupt – I feel rude doing so! But for me to be helpful I need to be able to take in everything you're saying and keep on top of it all. Would you mind if we press the pause button for a second? It sounds like you have a lot on, and I do want to acknowledge that and perhaps help think about how you can be best supported. But for now, would it be okay to spend ten minutes together focusing on your child's difficulties?

. . . .

Situation: Caregivers don't show up for the assessment.

Practitioner: In order for me to be able to help children, it's really important for me to meet with their parents. Sometimes parents have got things going on in their lives that make attending sessions difficult. Can we think through that or think about how to make it easier for you to come?

(It's also worth raising two or more non-attendances with your safeguarding leads. Some services record non-attendances as 'child not brought' to reflect the parents' responsibility in bringing their young person to appointments. Failing to meet that responsibility can in some cases become a safeguarding issue.)

. . . .

Situation: You've been working with a 14-year-old, and a parent or teacher asks you to attend a reintegration meeting after she's been temporarily excluded for wearing false eyelashes for the third time.

Practitioner: Thanks for inviting me but it doesn't sound as if it would be appropriate in terms of my role to attend this meeting. If you disagree and have reasons relating to the young person's emotional wellbeing that would mean my attendance was appropriate, then please do let me know them and I will discuss it with my team.

. . . .

It's normal to be unsure of how to respond to a variety of situations, and over time we develop more confidence. Do talk through sticky moments with your supervisor. Most of us have some degree of imposter syndrome and moments of doubt in this line of work are inevitable.

Try to always remember that the interventions we offer have been developed over several years and have had a huge amount of work and research put into them. Our job is delivering them as well as we can – and remember you are amazing for doing your best to do just that.

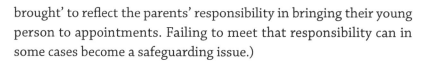 TRY IT OUT: meeting parents

Role play some of these situations with a colleague or your supervisor, and work out what responses feel right for you in your own words.

TAKE-AWAYS

▶ It's normal to feel apprehensive about working with parents and carers.

▶ Don't feel you have to answer any personal questions directly – you may want to boundary these.

▶ It isn't your role to help parents and carers with their own mental health.

▶ It's okay to politely try to steer a conversation back 'on topic'.

▶ Use supervision and try to be honest about any doubts or difficulties you are experiencing.

Part 2

PRACTICE ESSENTIALS

CHAPTER 6

Key Skills in Assessing and Goal Setting

Good assessment skills are crucial. In this chapter we'll look at how good timekeeping and a structured interview template will help, and outline why it's so important to ask our client if there's any aspect of their identity they think it'd be helpful for us to know. We look at a useful template for trying to understand how a difficulty is impacting on our client's life, and finally, we tackle goal setting, and how to transform a vague ambition into a smart, measurable and achievable goal.

THIS CHAPTER COVERS:

- Different kinds of assessment
- Questions that can help when thinking about identity
- Problem-focused assessment skills
- The value of 'externalising' a problem
- How to set 'SMART' goals

THE INITIAL ASSESSMENT AND SESSION ZERO

The initial assessment is the first meeting that either you or a more senior practitioner will have with the family or young person. It will help everyone learn more about the young person and decide what kind of support might be most useful. Your service should have a template that leads you through all the important areas, including:

- consent and confidentiality

- identity, culture and difference

- routine outcome measures

- family, school, friendships

- developmental history

- physical health, mental health in the family

- sleep and diet

- self-harm, suicidal ideation, any other harm or abuse

- drug/alcohol use

- other agency involvement and previous help

- description of the presenting problem

- initial goals

- any immediate care planning steps

- next steps.

It might seem like a daunting amount to cover. Sometimes it can't be done in one go – we can always carry questions over to the next session. It's important to stay client-centred and responsive because as someone once told me, the main aim of the first session is to get the client to come back for a second session!

Confusingly there are sometimes two different assessment sessions. After the initial assessment there's usually then a 'session zero' assessment where the practitioner gets acquainted with the client. During a session zero you get cracking with the psychoeducation, start to think about goals and discuss the next sessions. Including a session zero is obviously also a sneaky way of programme developers sneaking nine sessions into an eight-session model!

ONGOING ASSESSMENT

Once the initial assessment and session zero are out of the way, some aspects of assessment continue right through to the last session. Among other things, it involves thinking about: the family and the wider system; identity; risk; working out what the difficulty is; how likely the young person is to benefit from a particular intervention and also how useful the intervention proves to be. Let's call it 'assessing', instead of 'assessment', because it's a thread that never ends and something you do as you go along.

IDENTITY, FRONT AND CENTRE

It's essential we ask explicitly and warmly about someone's identity because it will impact on so many parts of their life. Let's think about some different aspects and how they might play out in someone's life and what would then be important to consider in our work.

Perhaps a young person holds some religious beliefs. They might be open to a cognitive behavioural understanding of low mood, whereas their parents might not accept such a viewpoint as it clashes with their own spiritual beliefs. This would be important to know so we can adapt the intervention to suit. Our client might have experienced racism while identifying as British and feeling judged by a grandparent for not observing some religious practices.

If a parent is under financial pressure they may not be able to afford a book you're recommending they read. They might not even have the money to pay for the bus travel to the community setting you hold your clinic in. How would you enquire about this in a sensitive way to ensure it wasn't a barrier for them to receive help?

A disability might also make it harder for someone to attend sessions. If it is a physical disability, it might have meant the young person has experienced discrimination in being unable to access their local tube station or go to the local theatre as easily as their friends, which may have made them feel pretty rubbish at times.

If you're working with a young person with anxiety who is struggling to get into some parts of town, we need to consider all the factors that might be at play before launching into graded exposure of any other kind of intervention. For example, some people may feel more threatened than others because of the colour of their skin or their ethnicity. And it's no wonder given the context of – among other things – the recent rise in anti-Semitic hate crime, or the fact that in the UK, as a young Black man you are 24 times more likely to be killed than a white man (Kumar, Sherman and Strang, 2020).

And if a therapist doesn't ask a 14-year-old about identity when they might be questioning their gender or sexuality, then they're potentially denying them the chance to think about this aspect of their identity, or being told about local lesbian, gay, bi, transgender, queer + (LGBTQ+) organisations.

CWP tutor Stuart Landsell suggests that 'a simple question about their preferred pronouns or comment from you letting the young person know your preferred pronouns may show them that you are open to have this discussion.'

Equally, CWP lecturer Kirsty Drysdale advises us to not specify gender when asking about others in the family. She remembers, 'When drawing a genogram, a young person mentioned his Mum's partner, and I asked what his name was – but the partner was female.'

We all have blind spots, and we've all been shaped by our experiences. But as mental health practitioners it's important we stay aware of our own privileges, assumptions and unconscious biases and develop our capacity to work with identity and difference. We are all works in progress, and in Chapter 10 we dive into some practical ways we can improve this aspect of our practice.

Frustrated with the lack of progress and change, assistant psychologist Glicínia Dansó came up with a brilliant question that we can all ask right at the start of getting to know someone:

'As a trust, we aim to be inclusive. Is there any aspect of your identity that would be useful for me to know? This can be used to enhance the way we work together.'

Clinical psychologist Sally McGuire also suggests we tell our clients there might be things they don't feel comfortable telling us at the start, but they may choose to share them as we get to know each other.

'I try to remember to ask them again further down the line,' Sally says. 'Similarly, if we are making a timeline of the client's important life events, at the start I will say: "If there is anything that has happened that you're not yet ready to talk about, then you can add a note and we can return to it later, if you feel ready to discuss it."'

▨ TRY IT OUT: asking about identity

Practise asking these questions in assessment role plays with a colleague. As you do so, try to maintain a warm, curious and wondering stance.

'What do you think is important for me to know about you, and what can I do to ensure I respect what you need?'

'Does your family have any religious or spiritual beliefs that really matter to you or other family members?'

'I'd be really interested to hear more about the traditions and celebrations that are important to you and your family or culture. Can you tell me more about any of them?'

'I wonder – what does your family make of the idea of mental health? What might they think about a family member talking about their own difficulties with someone else?' (adapted from Maiden, 2021)

UNDERSTANDING THE DIFFICULTY

Lives are messy, and it's rare to just have a single issue. So, while keeping identity in mind throughout our work, we also need to home in on the most pressing difficulty as we have limited time with our client and need to make our time together be as useful as possible.

Also, children and young people are normally referred in by teachers or parents and carers. It's rare for a young person to turn up at the door asking for help with a problem (although this should happen more often if good whole school approaches can destigmatise asking for help). We need to be mindful that a young person may have mixed thoughts and feelings about working with us.

As such, the onus is very much on us as practitioners to focus in on what it is we might be able to help with, bracket that, and then help our client set a SMART goal.

When trying to wrestle out a workable problem from a whirlpool of difficulties, we need to ask specific questions, for example:

'What is the main reason you came here today?'

'Are you looking for help with a particular problem?'

'What would you most like to work on?'

We also need to be careful not to locate the 'problem or issue' solely with the young person and to broaden out the lens to include the system and other contributing factors – more on this further on.

CO-MORBID DEPRESSION AND ANXIETY

Many young people experience both low mood and anxiety at the same time (two difficulties at once is known as 'co-morbidity'). How do we deal with this? First, ask the client which they think is the biggest problem for themselves, or which came first:

> 'Do you think you first felt depressed, then start feeling anxious about leaving the house, or did you first feel anxious, and then felt low about not being able to go out?'

Drawing out a timeline of the difficulties can be helpful with this.

It's quite common for a client to say they don't know, of course. If so, another approach could be to think about goals a little earlier in the assessment process. What would the client like to be different by the end of the intervention? What would they like to be doing that they're not at the moment? We can then open out that conversation and see what it is that's stopping them – whether it's more anxiety, or depression. Looking together at the results of the routine outcome measures can also help here. It may also be useful to discuss the case in supervision before going back to your client with a suggested plan. For more on what to do when both anxiety and depression are present, see Chapter 21.

THE 5WFIDO ASSESSMENT TOOL

To help narrow things further, the 5WFIDO tool (Table 6.1) is really handy. 5WFIDO stands for the who, what, where, why and when of the problem, as well as its frequency, intensity, duration and onset. Emotions are nebulous and it's a tool that enables us to start to nail down some realities around them in a way that is helpful for everyone. When you ask them, some of the questions might sound a bit silly, but it's amazing how often clients confound assumptions. It helps us get down to the detail.

Table 6.1: The 5WFIDO assessment tool

(After asking 'what is the problem', you don't have to ask the others in specific order)

What is the problem?

When is it a problem – when is it worse, when is it better?
(Times of day? Bed time? School breaks? Particular lessons?)

Where is it a problem?
(Is it worse at school/Mum's house/Dad's house/shopping centres/after-school clubs/other specific places?)

Who is it a problem with?
(particular friends/teachers, etc.?)

Frequency – how often does it happen? (how many times a week)
Intensity – when it happens, how bad is it from 0–10?
Duration – how long does it last in minutes or hours?
Onset – when did it start becoming a problem?

Why is it a problem?
(What does it get in the way of you doing? What did you used to enjoy that it's stopping you from enjoying? This is crucial for goal setting.)

▓ TRY IT OUT: role play using the 5WFIDO tool

Your colleague role plays being Asmah, a 12-year-old girl who hates eating in front of others. You role play being a CWP, using the 5WFIDO tool to find out more about her difficulty.

'I find this really hard to talk about, but I hate seeing people eat, and I hate being watched when I eat, too. I've never liked it, I find eating gross, and I eat on my own at home. It's become more of a problem since starting at secondary school. Instead of going to the canteen, I usually eat my sandwich in the toilets. If friends ask me to parties, I'll try to make sure I arrive after they've eaten, and make an excuse, like I'm feeling sick, or I'm vegan, if they offer me anything. It started when I saw someone throw up on the table next to us in a pizza restaurant. I think I was eight years old at the time. It was gross – the smell was disgusting. My Mum's really cool and understands and lets me eat on my own in the lounge most of the time. It's just me and her so it's easy at home.'

As the practitioner, what questions would you ask to help you get more specific about the problem?

EXTERNALISATION

One added therapeutic benefit of identifying a problem is that you can help a young person start 'externalising' it. It's the process of separating out the problem and starting to help a young person see it as separate from themselves. As narrative therapy inventor Michael White (White and Epston, 1990, p.55) wrote, 'the problem is the problem, the person is never the problem.'

Asmah's problem is stopping her from eating in front of others. Maybe we could call it the 'stops-me-eating' monster. However, her friends might think Asmah is *being a problem* by refusing to spend lunchtimes with them, and perhaps Asmah might see herself that way too.

If Asmah feels she has a problem she might get the sense it's temporary and she can do something about it. If she feels she is the problem, if feels permanent and unfixable.

So many of us feel personally to blame for our difficulties...none more so than the anxious kid whose parent is facing the threat of a school absence fine from the local authority, or the irritable, depressed teenager who's been labelled as challenging (or more likely, naughty) by everyone since he arrived in his new secondary school.

When a young person feels they are the actual problem, they're unlikely to have much hope or sense of agency for anything to change. That's why it's so important to help young people see themselves as the authors of their lives.

THE FORMULATION

As part of the assessment, you'll be doing a mini formulation, looking at how the problem has got established and maintained. In low intensity work we focus on identifying the 'vicious cycle' that is keeping the problem going. However, it still can be useful to use a timeline to identify any important life events or situations that may have triggered the difficulties such as relationship break-up, or a loss of a family member or pet, for example. It can also be helpful to think about any other contributory factors that might be playing a part in things not getting better – whether that's the stress of being in school, or dramas at home, or whatever. As mentioned in Chapter 5, using sticky notes is a nice way of adding to a formulation in an easy, graphic way where the young person is in control of what goes where.

GOAL SETTING

If you haven't heard of it before, the 'SMART' acronym stands for 'specific, measurable, achievable, realistic and time-limited' and it's the gold standard for good goal setting. Some prefer to say aim, plan or mission instead of goal – it's all good!

Naturally, young people might come up with general goals like 'I don't want to feel so crippled by anxiety' or 'I want to feel happy again.'

It's important to acknowledge how important such goals must feel. However, instead of setting a goal that measures the strength of a feeling, it is much better to focus on building towards a goal of doing something positive that a young person is currently not doing because of their emotional difficulty. This gives us a lot more to work with in a practical sense.

A goal like 'I would like to meet with two friends for half an hour every weekend' might sound a bit dry, but we know exactly what we're working towards.

The same principle applies when working with parents. A caregiver might say, 'I want Alex to be able to embrace new things and not be so anxious', but we'd need to get specific. If Alex was to embrace new things, what would he be doing? Would that include a sleep-over or a swimming lesson – what's the anxiety stopping him doing that he'd like to do?

If a young person says they want to be happy and free of anxiety, it's a starting point. Recognise it, say 'that's something we can work towards', but wonder with them if we can identify something measurable and achievable within the time frame you have. There's a saying – 'beware a dead person's goals'. Some degree of anxiety is inevitable in life. Watch out for a goal that a dead person could achieve more easily than someone who's alive!

A goal-setting conversation

Practitioner: I want to make these sessions really useful for you, Jared. You're taking time out of lessons to be here, and it's just got to be worth your while. What would you like to be different by the time we finish?

Client: Basically, I want to not feel so low and down all the time.

Practitioner: That must be really tough feeling like that. I wonder what you'd be enjoying if you weren't so low?

Client: I don't know. I've felt like this for so long.

Practitioner: Do you sometimes miss doing things you used to do?

Client: I used to love basketball.

Practitioner: Is that something you'd like to get back into?

Client: Yeah, I suppose so.

Practitioner: Shall we build a goal around that?

Client: Maybe.

Practitioner: It might sound a bit weird to work towards a goal of you playing basketball with your friends again, but it's something solid we can work towards, and we will find ways of helping you feel able to do it along the way. And if we're not getting there, step by step, then we can work out why and change tack.

Client: Yeah maybe.

It's not so much 'bad goal, good goal', but more taking the raw emotional difficulty, sifting through it, and finding some solid aims to work towards. And good goals have values linked to them...they matter because they matter to the person.

'I want to feel less anxious with my friends' could become 'I want to be able to go to the Christmas party with my friends and stay for an hour.'

'I want to get back into school' could be re-focused to 'I want to be in school for half a day every day by the last week of this term.'

'I want to not feel so sick when I see people eat' could become 'I want to be able to eat in a restaurant with my family by the end of next month.'

Also, goals might be hard for young people to come up with right at the start of your work. They may evolve, or become clearer, as you go. It's fine to have a preliminary goal, for example, 'I'd like to understand low mood better and know what steps I can take to help myself.' A couple of weeks later this could be followed with a goal such as 'I want a new routine and to get back into playing football three times a week.'

Goals can be short-term, mid-term, long-term or a mixture of all three. The client will have ideas about their goals, you will have your own ideas and if their parents or school staff are involved, they'll have their own ideas too. Stuart Lansdell advises practitioners to 'be mindful of this and ensure the young person has a strong voice in setting their goals.'

Goal based outcomes (Law and Jacob, 2015) are a way of measuring progress towards goals. Each week, we ask the client to mark on a line from 0 to 10 how far they feel they are towards achieving their goal. So, if my goal was to complete this book, I'd give myself about a 3 right now. In a month's time, I might, in my wildest dreams, have made it to a 5! These are usually done every session.

TRY IT OUT: goal setting

Give it a go with a friend. There are lots of SMART goal-setting sheets online to help prompt you for clarity as you flesh the goal out.

TAKE-AWAYS

▶ Use a comprehensive assessment questionnaire to help you stay organised in an initial assessment.

▶ Ask explicitly about your client's identity.

▶ Consider using the 5WFIDO model when doing an assessment of the problem.

▶ Hold in mind that 'the person is not the problem – the problem is the problem' and reinforce that viewpoint.

▶ Practise goal-setting conversations, taking a vague ambition and transforming it into a SMART goal.

CHAPTER 7

Ten Ways to Be a More Inclusive Practitioner

Inclusivity is so vital in mental health. Our differences, assumptions and privileges can have a huge effect not only on ourselves but also on dynamics within our work. These so often go unspoken and unacknowledged, but there's lots we can do about it to enhance our competency as practitioners. These are some quick, practical 'starter' suggestions as to how you can not only hold difference and diversity in mind, but actively work towards being a fully inclusive practitioner in a fully inclusive service.

THIS CHAPTER COVERS:

- Practical ways of improving access to all
- Considerations around language
- Ways to talk about the potential impact of racism and other hate crimes with a client

ASK ABOUT IT

Let's kick off with what's often the elephant in the room. You can do all the training you like and feel like you're the most knowledgeable, respectful person you know, but if you don't actually ask someone about their identity, it's all meaningless!

As covered in Chapter 6, remember to ask about identity in the assessment in a warm, curious manner, and continue to be curious about a person's experience throughout an intervention. Verna Myers (cited in Sherbin and Rashid, 2017) states that 'Diversity is being invited to the party. Inclusion is being asked to dance.'

It's particularly helpful to actively acknowledge rather than ignore the deep impact discrimination and minoritisation has on mental health. Perhaps ask, 'Have you or your family ever experienced any form of discrimination, or racism, or been the victim of a hate crime?'

During a session, we need to be culturally sensitive and enquire about how others might think about things similarly or differently to us. If you're working with a young person who's shown you that the older members of their family don't share the same views on mental health as them, then you need to think about this when looking at their back-up team with them. For example, you might say:

'I know you've put your Nan in your back-up team, and it sounds like you are really close with her. I wonder, what do you think your Nan would make of the term "low mood"? Would that fit with her religious and cultural beliefs? If not, I wonder if there's a better way of us talking about this stuff with her?'

And in the wake of really distressing events, it's appropriate to raise the likely impact of such ongoing injustice with a young person. It's highly likely that they will have been affected or even traumatised by news – and even if they haven't, it's good practice to check in with them, whatever their identity. This could be one approach:

'There's been some truly shocking events recently, with a number of Asian women attacked and a lot of hate crime happening on social media. It's been a really difficult time for a lot of people. Would it be okay to ask how it has been for you or if you've felt affected by this?'

So many people just don't consider how difference can make some people's lives much harder than others – as illustrated in Figure 7.1. Let's go out of our way to do the opposite!

Figure 7.1: Some aspects of people's lives are rarely thought about by others

USE FAMILY TREES

Family trees – also known as genograms – are fantastic graphic ways of trying to understand who is in a young person's life and build a picture of several generations on one page. If the client is comfortable to do so, they can also be a way of asking more about where different family members were born, what languages are spoken at home, the levels of religious observance and so on (Beck *et al.*, 2019). As supervisor Jo Lamprinopoulou puts it, 'family trees are an invitation to share more information in a thoroughly respectful manner.' It's a great way of 'kicking the ball about' without it becoming an uncomfortable inquisition. Something about a diagram being between you and the young person helps things feel less 'personal' too – you're discussing something that's out there on a table, or on a shared screen.

TRY IT OUT: family trees

Search for 'genograms' online for ideas of how to draw family trees. Then work with a colleague to explore their family history and con-nections. Perhaps preface the experiment with an open question like 'how would it be if we drew out your family tree together?' This will give them permission to say no or express any difficulties first. Stay open, supportive and curious.

CULTURALLY ADAPT THE THERAPY

Think with your supervisor and colleagues about how to adapt the work in order to make it as beneficial to the client as possible. Mir *et al.* (2015, as cited by Beck *et al.*, 2019) give a great example of how to do this well when offering behavioural activation to Muslim clients, with a lot of thoughtfulness put into how metaphors, language and religious parables can help with values-based behavioural change.

Equally, be mindful that some of our own norms might not apply to clients. David Trickey tells a story about working with a traumatised family from Kosovo, who would turn off the news if Kosovo was ever mentioned, and never talked about life back in their home country. David wondered about the value of talking about things with them, and said, 'Some say a problem shared is a problem halved.' Through their interpreter the father replied, 'In Kosovo, we say a problem shared is a problem doubled.'

TAKE CARE WITH PRONOUNS AND LABELS

Don't assume that someone is cis-gendered, non-binary, transgender or another gender identity – ask them their preferred gender identity. Take the same care when asking about relationships.

'Instead of asking someone if they've got a girlfriend or boyfriend, ask if they have a partner,' advises one young person. 'It's less intrusive, and less assuming in terms of sexuality.'

THINK ABOUT UNCONSCIOUS BIASES

Remember that you will, as a human being, be inclined to make assumptions based on your own experiences in life, and you will also, as a human being, apply your own frame of reference and unconscious biases to the young person you're working with. CWP tutor Lauren Hassan-Leslie states that, 'Acknowledging our own cultural beliefs and assumptions – including parts of ourselves we may be ashamed of, neglect or deny – is key to being able to have curious and sometimes difficult conversations about culture with our clients.'

But of course, it's not always easy. As racial justice educator Debbie Irving (cited in Cromar 2020) writes, 'it's so much easier for us to reject information that's uncomfortable than to actually create the kind of discomfort and dissonance in ourselves that we have to in order to take it in.'

Even all the things we see as 'our own' – our morals, values and political views – they're all intertwined and influenced by our culture, the country we grew up in, our families and so on.

As CWP tutor Kimberley Saddler says, 'Everyone has culture and if we can reflect on our own identities we can start to move away from the whole "white is the norm, BAME (Black, Asian and minority ethnic) is other" thing.'

The Social Graces model developed by Burnham (2012) is a really useful tool for starting to consider this stuff – and the following is a nice exercise to start exploring your own potential unconscious biases.

▨ TRY IT OUT: who do you spend time with?

Write down the names of five to ten people you spend the most time with. Then work through the columns in Table 7.1 for each person.

At the end, can you see any themes? Does the table reveal anything about who you're most comfortable with, and any blind spots you might have?

✱ Table 7.1: An exercise that may help you reveal your own unconscious biases

Name	Gender identity	Sexuality	Ethnicity	Religion	Political views

DON'T ASSUME ONE ASPECT OF IDENTITY IS MORE IMPORTANT THAN ANOTHER

As practitioners we have to be mindful of our own assumptions. If we are working with someone who identifies as trans, then that aspect of their identity may or may not play into their mental health – just as their new relationship, uncle's drinking problem, upcoming GCSE mocks or anything else going on in their life might.

'At times I've felt my disability has been a big thing, and I've not wanted it to be,' reflected one young person who uses a wheelchair. 'I went for help about something totally different.'

It's important not to make assumptions and follow the client's lead, actively seeking to understand and explore our client's self-defined identity.

THINK ABOUT LANGUAGE

Diversity and inclusion consultant Laurelle Brown (2020) advises us to be mindful of our language when talking about 'minorities' and refer instead to people as they identify. Laurelle advises that we stop using the BAME moniker as it currently stands. By being a 'catch-all' phrase, it reinforces the otherness and minoritisation of anyone who isn't white, and positions whiteness as the norm. She argues that we should change the BAME acronym from being the commonly held interpretation of 'Black, Asian and minority ethnic' to 'Black and minoritised ethnicities'. By verbalising 'minoritised', the second description helps us refocus on both the truth and structure of a society where a white majority has minoritised, and continues to minoritise, other ethnicities. Laurelle's point serves as a reminder for us to always ask clients what words they prefer to use in discussions about identity. Jo Lamprinopoulou reflects that what matters most is that 'we create opportunities to invite these conversations into the therapeutic space.'

DEVELOP YOUR SOCRATIC DIALOGUE SKILLS

What can really help, in practice, is following the principles of 'Socratic dialogue' (more on this in Chapter 9). When it's working well, a client's responses are a surprise and a delight, because we are getting past our own assumptions, and discovering, with the client, how things really are for them.

I had some sessions of CBT to help me with some lingering shame I felt over my sexuality, which, coupled with my tendency to over-think, was contributing to anxiety. My straight therapist was gently curious about my experience, and asked interesting questions, often prefacing them with comments like, 'I know this might be a really dumb thing to ask, but...'. The honesty and 'let's pick our way through this' nature of the conversation helped me sort the woods from the trees in terms of my own internalised homophobia. Of course, there are still huge amounts of homophobia in society, but my therapist helped me see that at least some of my anxious thinking and shame were rooted in past experiences and belonged there, and not in the present. I was thankful for my therapist's honesty, and it didn't matter a jot to me that he wasn't a 'sexuality expert' or hadn't had similar experiences of shame himself. As Socrates said, 'an honest man is always a child' – and my therapist was humble enough to put himself in that place.

KEEP TRAINING

As part of your continuous professional development – and particularly if you become aware of any blind spots – seek out further training. Research (Strauss *et al.*, 2021) has shown that this can be really beneficial for treatment outcomes for minoritised people. There is evidence that healthcare professionals who've had specific training on transgender issues tend to exhibit more affirmative and positive attitudes (Riggs and Bartholomaeus, 2016). This and other research show that it is the cultural sensitivity of the therapist that matters most – not necessarily being the same ethnicity or having a similar identity. It's the openness and curiosity that counts. One nice way of being curious is to say, 'I don't know much about X, but perhaps you can help me understand more?'

Of course, for some clients, ethnic and gender matching can sometimes be helpful – so it's important to be curious about this. But above all, the aim is to work towards an attitude of cultural humility, where we learn to 'walk beside or with another' (Hoskins, 1999), actively seeking to become educated about another person's culture and identity and exploring what we don't know with a warm curiosity.

Saiqa Naz (2021, p.21) puts it nicely. 'I don't pretend to know any-thing about all communities and neither do I ignore it,' writes Saiqa. 'I have learnt to sit with it, own it and create space for it in my sessions and personal development. Using supervision is important here.'

ACTIVELY REACH OUT

Wellbeing services should be engaged in making sure they reach every member of the community. Equality of access is enshrined in legis-lation (Equality Act, 2010). We also need to get better at effectively communicating what our services can offer (Beck *et al.*, 2019). This means getting out there and forming relationships with community and religious groups and organisations – whether that's LGBTQ+ (les-bian, gay, bisexual, transgender, queer and others) groups, mosques or youth projects – and working together, using interpreting services where needed.

Jo Lamprinopoulou stresses the importance of recognising that the expertise lies with the group that we are reaching out to. 'We need to try to organise awareness training by prominent leaders within communities,' she says. 'It's an opportunity to understand a community from within the eyes of the community and build working relationships.'

Kimberley Saddler agrees. 'CWPs are really well placed to work in youth hubs where you see a hugely diverse group of young people attending,' she says.

And don't forget the stuff that can be easily overlooked. Services should make their stance on equality, diversity and inclusion really visible: posters and websites should reflect the service's values.

TAKE-AWAYS

► By asking about identity and difference and using practical tools like family trees we can keep it front and centre in our practice.

► A warm, curious stance can help a client feel more able to express how things are for them.

► We all have our own unconscious bias and assumptions, and discussing these in supervision helps stop them from impacting on the quality of our work.

► Our services should actively try to engage all communities and reach out to people of all walks of life.

CHAPTER 8

A Good Session Is Like a Three-Course Meal

When you go for a meal out, you expect to be given a menu so you can see what's on offer. A really good waiter will check in on how things are going, too. It's the same with our work – we need to find out what our client wants and make sure they're happy with things as we rumble through the session. For some it can feel counter-intuitive (and business-like) to be talking about agenda setting and feedback monitoring, but they are integral to the cognitive behavioural way of working.

THIS CHAPTER COVERS:

- Why agenda setting and asking for feedback matters
- How to talk about an agenda and how to set one
- The use of 'session rating scales'
- Why we ask clients what they'll remember from each session

Agenda setting is particularly critical when we have so few sessions with a young person, parent or carer. We need to make sessions as useful as possible. If they're not set up as clinical appointments, an hour can quickly drift by in a meandering conversation. The structural elements of a session are also helpful in making sessions even more collaborative and client-centred: the young person or parent is at the heart of it all and the structure helps maintain the focus firmly on helping them towards their goals. If you're a fan of person-centred counselling founder Carl Rogers (1951) and share his philosophy that humans will naturally heal and develop given the right conditions, this style might feel too directive. If so, perhaps it'd help to think of these structural elements as 'useful conditions'?

Let's think of a session as being like a three-course dinner. The starter is your agenda setting and check-in, then you get into the main course – the content. The dessert is your chance to recap on any home practice tasks and a time to ask for feedback.

It should go a little something like this:

Starter
Welcome
Agenda setting
Check-in and routine outcome measures

Main course
Review progress over last week
This week's content and discussion
Agree home practice tasks

Dessert
Recap on the session – what's been important?
Recap on home practice tasks
Ask for feedback + Session Feedback Questionnaire
Write it all up

HOW TO TALK ABOUT AGENDA SETTING

At the start of each appointment, it's important to spend a couple of minutes agreeing with your client what you're going to cover. You need to be honest about what you plan to cover, and also ask your client what they want to bring and what is most important to them. You don't have to call it an agenda of course, you could say something like: 'Before we delve into things, how about we spend a couple of minutes making a list of what we want to cover in the next hour? Would that be useful?'

A lot of young people don't find it easy to come up with ideas. That's fine. One approach for dealing with this is to respond with: 'It's totally fine if you don't have any particular ideas. Here are the bits I reckon would be good to go through... What's most important to you? Anything you'd like to add? What order shall we do them in?'

After you've written down the agenda together and allocated time for each piece, you could also agree who will keep time. You could consider asking the young person to take responsibility for this – 'Hey have you got a phone – would you mind just keeping an eye on the time for us as we go along?'

This will increase the collaborative nature of your session – it makes it less of a 'teacher-pupil' dynamic where the practitioner is seen as being in charge. As the practitioner, you could also then ask, 'How are we doing for time?' every now and again during the session. And of course, it makes it a tad easier for you as you have one less job to do.

GETTING FEEDBACK

When clearing the plates from each course, a good waiter will ask their customer how they found their food. They'll also ask for general feedback at the end of the meal too. We need to do the same. Get into the practice of asking your client how the session is going and getting final feedback at the end. So – after the 'starter', you could perhaps ask: 'Just checking – how was setting the agenda – did we get everything in that you wanted to?' We should repeat this kind of check-in after each agenda item – for example, 'Is everything clear about the home practice you think would be useful?'

And then at the end of the session, it's really important our client gets the chance to rate their session. You could say something like:

'I want to make sure these sessions are as useful as possible for you. Would it be okay to ask you a few questions about how this one has gone? Please do be as honest as possible because if there are things I can be doing better or differently that you'd prefer, I'd love you to help me learn how.'

TRY IT OUT: check-ins

In your next session, make a point of making at least five interim 'check-ins' during the course of the session to see how your client is finding things. This is an excellent way of improving client-centred practice.

Feedback questionnaires vary between services. The Session Rating Scales (Miller, Duncan and Johnson, 2000) require a license and include four questions that ask the client to mark a line from 0 to 10 on how much they agree with how respected and understood they've felt, whether you've worked on what they wanted to cover, whether your approach was a good fit, and overall how well the session went. A good alternative that doesn't require a license is the Session Feedback Questionnaire. Whichever you use, these questions are a nice way of finding out how the client has found the session, so you can work together on making any changes that are needed for the next one. You might feel nervous asking your client to rate how well it's gone, but you'll get used to it pretty quickly if you just build it in as a normal part of the session.

Be confident enough to encourage clients to rate the session poorly if that's how they feel. It should matter to you that the sessions are useful, and it's okay to tell a client this as a reason for why you want them to be honest. Low intensity interventions are brilliant vehicles for change, but they often need repairs as you head off down the road. The feedback scales help us work out when we need to get the jump leads out to restart the car, or take a different turn, or change our driving style.

ASKING FOR TAKE-AWAYS

At the end of a session, ask the young person what they think will be important to remember from the session. It takes only 20 minutes before we forget half of what we've learnt, as discovered by Ebbinghaus (1880; see Murre, 2015) in his pioneering memory recall experiments. Encouraging a young person to recall what their session take-aways are will help them 'stick' – getting them to write it down is even better. As Nick Grey (2021) says, 'if you don't write it down, it didn't happen.' It's also really interesting feedback for us as practitioners. Nine times out of ten a client's take-aways are not what we'd expect!

When working with more complex cases, I'll often email the client a summary of what we've discussed and the agreed next steps, but in low intensity work most young people are okay to write stuff down as they go. It can be tempting to take over to speed things up, but clients often develop a stronger sense of ownership and connection to the learning and action points if they write them up themselves.

There are a few creative ways to scribble down take-away points. During my CBT training lecturer Miltos Bikakis used to ask us to make a quick drawing summarising what we'd learnt at the end of each lesson. He'd tell us to draw a suitcase (see Figure 8.1), stick the lesson's content on the baggage label, then write or draw three things we'd learnt inside it. An alternative is to give your client an A5 card to scribble stuff down on. Maybe you could do one of these now?

Figure 8.1: What are you taking away from this session?

CHAPTER 9

Tips for Good Therapeutic Conversations with Young People

A CAMHS manager once told me that some practitioners have an 'x factor' in being able to engage with young people. 'You either have it or you don't,' she said. I disagree – I think it's something we can all keep working towards, wherever we're starting from. Yes, it takes lots of practice and commitment to develop good therapeutic skills, and I know I'm often getting it wrong. Thankfully, psychologists have researched and evaluated a series of demonstrable qualities that we can keep in mind and use to check in on our own progress (Fuggle, Dunsmuir and Curry, 2012). That's why reviewing videos of our sessions is so helpful, however cringe-making it may be. These qualities form the basis for the EMHP and CWP competency frameworks. What follows are some suggestions on what to focus on in order to develop these competencies.

THIS CHAPTER COVERS:

- The things that young people really value in practitioners
- What a good 'working alliance' means
- Why checking in frequently and pacing matter
- The value of curiosity, encouragement, wonder, creativity, empathy and playfulness
- Why getting things wrong is okay when you own up to it

- What 'Socratic dialogue' is
- How to work with the power differential

WHAT REALLY MATTERS

A recent survey reveals that what matters most to children and young people when they come for help is slightly different from what many have assumed. According to Berry, Law and Ryan (2021), children, young people and parents who attend CAMHS services say that what they really appreciate in their practitioner is 'a sense of reliability', 'a sense of trust' and being 'non-judgemental'. Openness of communication, an acceptance of a young person's difficulties and being consistent are important, too.

Historically, many therapists have been influenced by the seminal work of Carl Rogers, the founder of person-centred therapy. Rogers (1951) posited that empathy, unconditional positive regard and congruence are the cornerstones of both a strong therapeutic relationship and effective therapy.

Since then, a lot has been made of the importance of the therapeutic alliance. Some research suggests it's a common denominator for successful therapy regardless of the therapist's theoretical orientation (Horvath and Luborsky, 1993). 'It's the relationship that heals' is a well-known quote from Irvin Yalom (1989, p.112).

But seriously, is that not a whole load of pressure?

'Here's a depressed 15-year-old – you've got eight sessions, off you go, build a relationship that heals!'

'Okay, I'll do my best!'

Yet that's the implicit request within many of the referrals given to school counsellors. I know all too well the pressure you can feel when you're working on the basis that your main tool is quickly building fantastic rapport with your client and then some kind of magical healing relationship. And, funnily enough, it doesn't always work out that way.

In low intensity work, instead of calling the dynamic between therapist and client the 'therapeutic alliance', its termed a 'working alliance' – representing a subtle but important shift. The working alliance is seen as more the glue that helps get the rest of the work done, rather than the active ingredient in itself. Aaron Beck *et al.* (1979) said the relationship should act as a kind of laboratory for change. As Helen Kennerley points out, it's 'the nature of the patient's participation in treatment that is the strongest predictor of outcome' (2014, p.33). And treatment trials in adult work bear this out to be true: they show that CBT combined with a good working relationship delivers better results than a good therapeutic alliance alone (Roth and Fonagy, 2005).

Of course, a good working alliance is really important, but hopefully the above puts a tweak on why it matters and what helps create one. We don't have to create some kind of healing bond. Instead, just remember what the research tells us: that reliability, trust and a non-judgemental partnership with boundaries are key to good therapeutic relationships (Berry, Law and Ryan, 2021). And that's no bad thing when we've got just eight sessions!

Let's look now at what can help us create a helpful working alliance in as short a time as possible.

TALK NORMALLY!

Most importantly, we need to learn to talk with a child or young person in a way they understand. That means thinking carefully about using technical words like intervention, formulation, maintenance factor, presentation. When you start in mental health work, you may feel a bit intimidated hearing lots of psychological jargon and acronyms, and by and large they're fairly meaningless to most people, and potentially confusing too. I know they can help bolster our own sense of emerging professional competence (yes, I've been there). If you have to use technical terms, then enquire about their understanding of them as you do so. So, for example, if talking about confidentiality, maybe ask your client, 'Hey, do you know about confidentiality? What does the word mean to you?'

CHECK HOW THEY'RE DOING

Try to be sensitive to their developmental level and if in doubt, ask if they get it or not! On that, try to steer clear of closed questions like, 'Does that make sense?' I have to work really hard to stop myself saying that, and instead try to ask 'What do you make of that?', which encourages a more reflective response. If a young person can tell you what they make of something, you can really check out their understanding of it. After all, how many of us have sat there in class just nodding away while the maths equations fly right over our heads? I've got a friend who's into cars, and as soon as he starts trying to explain pistons or engines to me, I go straight back into nodding mode, just wishing he'd hurry up and finish the explanation. Which he never does.

ONE BALL AT A TIME

Figure 9.1: When explaining stuff, take it point by point and check for reception frequently. Try to serve one ball at a time

If a conversation was like a game of tennis, you wouldn't serve your conversation partner ten balls over the net all at once (Figure 9.1). Give them time to receive each ball and knock it back at you. If you're giving psychoeducation or information, just give them one or two bits of information, then check for understanding. That means talking for 15–20 seconds then checking in with them. Try it out. It might feel a bit artificial at first but get into the practice of it.

After you've given each bit of information, ask something like:

What do you make of that?

How does that sit with you?

Dumb question, but are there any similarities between what I've said and what you experience?

BE CURIOUS, NOT CLEVER

'Adopting a non-expert, tentative stance' is how the EMHP competencies framework puts it (Anna Freud Centre, 2020) – but I think we can go one better. 'Be curious, not clever' is great advice from clinical psychologist Nick Grey (2021). We need to be genuinely interested in the young person's life and perspective. Try to keep a little bit of room for this, even when you feel the pressure of getting through an entire session's content. Sometimes when reviewing EMHP videos, a client can be yawning away, yet the EMHP feels so much pressure to crack on they don't pick up on it. Don't be that EMHP!

Also, it's so much easier to talk to someone when we feel they're genuinely interested in us. My first supervisor, Leslie Ironside, used to always advocate for curiosity. He said he was once asked what kind of therapist would be best for someone's child, and he replied, 'the one who's most genuinely interested in them'.

Peter Fonagy, CEO of the Anna Freud Centre, tells a lovely story that illustrates this point (Doward, 2019). Peter arrived in the UK aged 17 years old, a refugee from Hungary. Feeling utterly depressed, Peter went to the Anna Freud Centre for therapy.

In his first session, Peter's only animated moment was when he told his therapist about his new car. In truth, it was a beaten-up old rust bucket, but the therapist got out of her chair, walked to the window and said, 'Peter, that is a wonderful car.'

'Recognising my pride in it, seeing that what I needed was someone else appreciating my excitement, that really helped me trust my therapist,' recounts Peter. 'It made her a legitimate source of advice, someone I would take seriously.'

BE A COACH

A young person may have had a mixed experience of school and teachers, so it's important we give extra encouragement and actively demonstrate we're on their side. This is even more important when working via phone or online. You might sound a bit ridiculous doing it at first, but dropping in, 'you're doing really well', or 'well remembered', along with lots of nodding and smiling, are active ways of compensating for the non-verbal cues we naturally give when we're physically present with someone.

▨ TRY IT OUT: be more encouraging

In your next online session, aim to be 50 per cent more encouraging than you would normally. Our brains are often addled with trying to get through the session material, and it can be so easy to forget how important praise and encouraging words are for young clients.

DO SOME WONDERING

When we're working with someone who is struggling with anxiety or low mood hold in mind how these difficulties can affect the person we're with, and wonder about that with them. Peter Fuggle teaches 'mentalisation' – an art which involves wondering what's going on in the mind of another. During my own training, we were shown a CBT video with Peter working with a depressed 14-year-old. It was their first session, early on, and the dialogue went like this:

Peter: One thing I know about depression is it can slow our brains down, make them go all foggy, and make it really hard to take stuff in.

[Client nods]

Peter: I wonder if that might happen for you sometimes?

[Client nods]

Peter: And I wonder too, maybe I could check in to see how you're doing every now and again, and if you can't take what I'm saying in, could you let me know?

In this simple exchange, Peter imparts some psychoeducation on the effects of depression to the young person. He also normalises these effects and shows some kindness and empathy while doing it. It's just a gentle tweak to wonder about something happening rather than stating it as a fact, and it allows the client to reflect and report back. Last, Peter also strengthens the working alliance by saying that this stuff is so important to him that he'd like to check in with the client about it every now and again – and asks permission to do that. It's magic stuff.

Figure 9.2: Stay curious and ask lots of 'I wonder'
questions as you explore a client's world

We can use the 'I wonder' approach in lots of ways – it's a bit like dropping a pebble in a lake and seeing what ripples emerge:

'I wonder what it's like feeling under so much pressure with exams, and if that doesn't make other aspects of life really hard for you at times?'

'I wonder if us talking about this stuff might be really difficult for you right now, as I noticed you're a little quieter than at the start of the session. Have I got that right?'

'I wonder how this session's going for you as we've covered a lot so far – is the pacing okay?'

'I wonder what it's like talking to a man about this stuff? I mean, I might be a similar age to the teacher you find really difficult.'

BE CREATIVE

Play around with different methods for different young people to see what works – talking, drawing, texting, quizzes, cartoons, metaphors and so on. Use your natural strengths. I'm rubbish at art but love trying to use analogies to explain things. Don't beat yourself up for what you can't do. Manuals are a great tool for creativity as they give space for both writing and doodles and drawing. If you're in a school, then whiteboards are really handy. If you're working online then being able to share your screen will be essential, and you can use different programmes to draw and be creative through different platforms.

'Above all, ask the young person what works best for them,' advises EMHP supervisor Sam Thompson.

BE EMPATHIC

After seven years of working as a qualified psychotherapist in primary schools, I failed my first CBT video submission for not showing enough empathy. My client was describing being bullied in the playground, and instead of stopping and validating with 'that sounds really difficult', or 'how horrible for you' I was too busy thinking of how we would formulate the experience using a Five Ps model. I didn't come across at all well. Don't be like me. Be like Carl Rogers.

CWP programme director Vicki Curry says that 'the way to demonstrate empathy is through listening and validating.' She suggests, 'Try it out with a colleague, record it and play it back to yourself. The number one thing I wish all our trainees did more of in their video submissions is demonstrating lots of empathising.'

GET IT WRONG, AND OWN UP TO IT

Now and again it's actually really helpful to acknowledge if you don't feel you're doing a good job, or don't know something, or have messed up. By doing so, you're modelling that it's okay to make mistakes. I mean, how bad would our mental health be if we felt we always had to get everything right all the time? (Oh, hello my own mental health, nice to see you again!) Most importantly, if you think you've misunderstood something, check it out. Try saying things like:

'I might be totally wrong here, but are you saying you're more anxious in some classes than others?'

'I think I didn't do a good job of explaining that – shall I try drawing it out instead?'

'Sorry, I don't think I got that right, could you say that again?'

BE A BUMBLING DETECTIVE

A good CBT therapist is brilliant at 'Socratic dialogue'. It's a way of talking and asking questions that encourages the student to learn their own answers for themselves and it's a 'cornerstone of cognitive therapy' (Padesky, 1993). As Socrates said, 'wonder is the beginning of wisdom.' When we talk in this way, we don't ask super-clever questions that we think we already know the answers to – instead we kind of bumble along, asking questions that might even seem a bit silly, feeling our way though. Aaron Beck, the father of cognitive therapy, reckoned that the TV detective Columbo had it about right, bumbling along on a hunch. Socratic questions might include:

'This might sound like a really stupid question, but...'

'Can you tell me more about the difficulty?'

'When you felt like that, did you label yourself as anything?'

'What went through your mind when that happened?'

The great thing about Socratic dialogue is that it's not about 'changing minds, but guiding discovery' as Padesky says (1993). It helps keep us in that place of 'not quite knowing' – the tentative, non-expert stance as encouraged in the EMHP and CWP competencies. We try to keep the conversation 'liminal' – a lovely word that Michael Rosen (2021) often uses in his writing workshops. It means a space or moment between two worlds or on the edge of one world but not quite in another.

We're sticking with and exploring that gap in the minds of ourselves and the young person as we try to understand them better. And by encouraging the young person to think more for themselves, helping us out with the answers, there's more opportunity to loosen things up and invite opportunities to change. We only need to be in this mode for parts of a session – of course it makes sense to be more didactic and teacher-like when we need to impart some specific new knowledge or skills to a young person (for example, teaching a grounding technique).

REMEMBER THE POWER DIFFERENTIAL

Even if you're not twice the size or age of the young person in front of you, remember there's a huge power difference between you (adult, professional, badge-wearer) and them (child or young person). It's often not even the young person's idea to come for help. From the off we need to be explicit that we will be respectful of their choice to come or not. The BABCP's *CBT with Children, Young People and Families: BABCP Good Practice Guide* (Maddox *et al.*, 2021) encourages practitioners to be up front with young people about this. The guide quotes a young person as reporting that 'in my first session, my therapist said, "if you don't like it, or me, tell someone"…for the person in the room to say that made me feel like I did have a choice.'

Sometimes we might need to steer a session back on track. Some kids tell amazing stories and jump from one thing to the next. Being mindful of the power differential in the room, you might have to say something like, 'Hey I feel a bit rude interrupting – I'm sorry! It's just I know how important the goals you set for yourself are, and I wondered…what do you think if we get back to focusing on that, and what you wanted to cover in the agenda? What do you reckon?'

Berry, Law and Ryan (2021) also found that young people want practitioners to be transparent about the fact that they'll have to pass on concerns at times to their parents and carers. If confidentiality isn't explained well, or young people feel practitioners have gone behind their back, this can be very damaging.

BE PLAYFUL

At times, it's okay to bring your natural humour into sessions. Psychologist Dan Hughes advocates a 'PACE' approach, using playfulness, acceptance, curiosity and empathy. It's more than fine to introduce playful approaches to serious problems. Used sensitively, moments of lightness often help when talking about dark stuff.

Advanced skills: the downward arrow technique

Once something important comes to the surface, we can also use 'the downward arrow technique' to help us deepen our understanding and hone our next steps to be most useful for the client. It can feel awkward asking the client to stick with the difficulty and tell us more about it – so it helps to bumble about a bit as we do it in the Socratic style. It can really flesh out the client's experience and what's truly difficult about it for them, and also how it might have impacted how they think about themselves. Possible questions could include:

And what's the worst part of it all for you?

How did it feel in your body?

And what does that say about you?

What do you imagine the others thought when that happened?

In your mind, what were you most frightened of that might have happened next?

Because these are quite blunt questions, it can be less jarring if we add a bit of a preface. For example, 'This might sound like a really dumb question, but I'm going to ask it anyway...what was so bad about that for you?'

Here's an example of a CWP using the downward arrow technique:

CWP: Feeling sick with nerves when walking into school sounds awful. I wonder – what thoughts go through your mind when you're feeling like that?

YP: That I can't cope, I hate school, and I'm weird because all my friends can get in fine.

CWP: Those sound like really difficult worries and thoughts. This might sound like a silly question, but what's the worst bit for you in particular?

YP: Thinking I'll never get better.

CWP: How horrible for you. Thanks for sharing that, I now understand a little better how difficult this is for you and how important it must feel for things to get better for you.

We could then move into some normalising and psychoeducation, for example: 'When we feel anxious it's so normal to have anxious thoughts like these.' Or 'Anxiety in our tummies sometimes feels like a fire, and our thoughts are like the smoke rising out of the fire – it's all linked up.'

You might also think of exceptions, for example a time when the client was able to manage their anxiety and keep doing something (maybe a primary school Christmas performance, or a football game?) and it went down over time. You can then start thinking about what could be tried differently in those moments of anxiety and think together about coping strategies.

When using this kind of questioning, it's important to do a bit of scaffolding and reflecting, be attuned to the client and definitely avoid anything that is erring towards an interrogation. Eastwood *et al.* (2016) have written a really good guide to developmentally appropriate Socratic dialogue with children and young people that's well worth a read – as is Helen Kennerley's 'Socratic Method' booklet.

TAKE-AWAYS

▶ A good working alliance is the foundation of good practice.

▶ Remember to check in frequently, and be mindful of pacing – particularly with anxious and depressed clients.

▶ Being encouraging and giving lots of praise is particularly valued when working online, where other cues aren't so obvious.

▶ Wondering, being curious, being empathic, staying with the client... these are skills that we keep developing throughout a lifetime!

▶ Always remain professional, but remember the power difference.

▶ Read up on Socratic dialogue to develop your skills further.

CHAPTER 10

Some Creative Activities to Improve Access and Engagement for All

There's an endless number of ways to help oil the wheels of engagement and ease the explaining of psychological ideas. And when we consider neurodiversity, it's so important we make sessions accessible and useful for all.

THIS CHAPTER COVERS:

- Games and activities to help early engagement
- Metaphors that can aid with psychoeducation
- Other activities that can assist, including pie charts

EARLY ENGAGEMENT ACTIVITIES
The squiggle game

Invented by psychoanalyst Donald Winnicott, the squiggle game is a fantastic way of building some initial rapport with a client in a first session. It's also something we can teach parents and kids to do together as a fun activity. Because it doesn't involve much talking it's particularly useful when working with shy young people, and it's a way of seeing each other's imagination at work and getting to know each other in a playful way.

It's simple. Grab a sheet of paper and draw a simple squiggle on it (even a zigzag will do). Then pass your pen to the child or young person and ask them to make a picture out of it, by developing your squiggle into a shape. Once done, you have to guess what it is. You can then start a new drawing – letting the young person draw the squiggle and then you do the hard work after. I'm sure a psychoanalyst would have a field day interpreting the drawings but what's the point? It's basically just a bit of fun to help get our working relationship off to a good start. Having said that, if a young person really struggles to engage with it, that might tell you something about their level of anxiety, or perhaps indicate some neurodiversity that will need considering as you go.

Would you rather

Would you rather have a bath in baked beans, or shower in cabbage soup? Would you rather fight 100 chicken-sized horses, or one horse-sized chicken? Would you rather have a dog's head on your own body, or have your own head on a dog's body? Take it in turns to come up with scenarios and talk about the alternatives together. You could have a set of cards with different scenarios to turn over and respond to. It's a nice ice breaker!

The yes, no game

First person to say 'yes' or 'no' is out! Try to have a normal conversation, throwing in the occasional trick question to catch the other person out. It's actually really difficult. Perhaps not best done during a formal assessment. But it does help lighten the mood at times at the start of other sessions.

Mallet's mallet

This is a word association game first devised by TV presenter Timmy Mallet, and most familiar to children of the 1980s. It goes like this: one person says a word, and the other has to say the first word that comes into their head that's associated with it. For example, 'Australia', 'kangaroo', 'poo', 'toilet' and so on. Or at least that's how my mind works. Any hesitation or repetition and you're out. In the original version on TV, Timmy Mallet would whack the losing player's head with his large foam mallet. Not advised during our work.

Five things

Draw around your outstretched fingers on a piece of A4, and then tell the young person five things about yourself, writing them down on each finger. Then ask them to do the same. Your topics should be fairly generic (favourite food, animal, TV series, etc.), and can act as a prompt for them if they're feeling shy or anxious.

METAPHORS AND ANALOGIES

Pets and animals

Talking about pets and animals can really help with psychoeducation. For example, with anxiety, cats are my go-to animal (see Figure 10.1). Ask a young person if they've ever seen how a cat puffs itself up when it sees a strange cat outside to make itself look bigger and scarier. We can compare this with what our human bodies do when we're stressed. We can also talk about cats seeing their reflection in a window and getting freaked out and acknowledge that our minds and bodies react to both real and imagined threats in the same way.

Trains of thought

Sometimes young people find it hard to stay on topic, and the conversation can 'jump about the tracks'. To be honest, if you've got an active mind there are a lot more interesting things to talk about than your anxiety! Rambling chats can get in the way of working towards a client's goal, though. We can say, 'Hey, my old brain can't keep up with your active one and all its twists and turns! I wonder if what's going on is a bit like this…'

We can then draw one train track going up one side of a bit of paper, and another going up the other (see Figure 10.1). One is relatively straight, and the other is going left and right, and round in a circle over a bridge and then taking a fork to the right. This can start a conversation about how if we were two trains, we'd like the tracks to try to stay nice and close so we can keep travelling together in the same direction. 'Does your mind ever feel like the twisty-turny track? And if so, would it be okay to ask gently to bring our trains of thought back closer together?'

ready for action!

*Figure 10.1: Train tracks can be a useful metaphor as we try
to 'stay on track' during a conversation. Animals and their
responses are great as we engage in psychoeducation*

TikTok vs Netflix

Another way of talking about 'topic-jumping' is to compare watching
lots of back-to-back 15-second TikTok videos with a Netflix show. Say,
'Look, I'm a bit slower than you and sometimes I can't keep up when
the videos keep changing! Would you mind if we try to stay on one
topic for a little longer to give me a chance to keep up?'

Video games

Video games make for fantastic metaphors. When you're playing a
video in 'story mode', your progress gets automatically saved at regular
checkpoints. This is a good metaphor for progress – we don't always
notice it happen, but we're never starting the game again absolutely
from scratch. Equally, lots of games have levels ending with a boss level
– we can use these as metaphors for the steps a young person is taking
towards their ultimate goal. In a shooter game, coping strategies could
be described as our weapons, and rewards as new 'skins', and so on.

Washing machines

Washing machines are also great. We can draw out a washing machine, and use the circular window for our formulation template, putting three sticky notes on it to describe the thoughts, feelings and behaviours that happen during a vicious circle. Washing machines also go into a 'spin cycle', making loads of noise. Some feel like they're about to skip off across the kitchen floor! This is a good metaphor for what our minds do when we start ruminating or worrying excessively – our minds turn round and round like the drum of a washing machine and we can't find the off button. Washing machines also have heavy bricks at their base to keep them stable – that's what makes them so heavy to carry. We can use these as a metaphor for the people who keep us grounded and safe – a bit like our 'back-up team'. This idea is particularly helpful when working with young people who've been though a lot in their lives – including those in care. We can also use the bricks to describe coping tools to help us when our minds go into a whir.

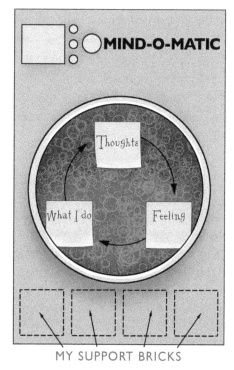

Figure 10.2: The washing machine metaphor

OTHER IDEAS

Drawing

Rather than giving young people endless handouts (often black and white, generally a bit dull) we can increase participation and engagement by encouraging clients to get drawing and creating their own resources. A worry tree is a classic example – it's quite fun to draw out a classic Christmas tree, stick the worry in a Christmas star at the top, and write down the unique steps the young person will take to sort their worries out themselves underneath.

Videos

There are lots of excellent animations online that do a great job of explaining concepts like the fight, flight, freeze response. Usually it's a case of the shorter, the better – look for videos that are age appropriate, and three minutes long maximum.

Chairwork

Sometimes it can be nice to 'externalise' a problem and imagine it sitting somewhere else in the room. You could say, 'Imagine your depression is sitting over there on that chair. What does it look like?'

You can then wonder together about how best to relate to and manage this aspect of their lives. That's the shortest description of chairwork ever, and while not a part of low intensity training, it can definitely be integrated into our work.

Pie charts

Draw out a circle on a piece of paper and tell your client you're really interested in exploring something they've just said to you further. It gets the content out onto a piece of paper (or a shared screen) between you and enables further reflection on values, change and more. We can use pie charts for loads of things to get to know someone better, for example:

> Using two pie charts, how big is the depression now, compared with a year ago?

> Thinking about friends, family, school and sport, how much space would each take up on a pie chart?

Of the people who you live with at home, who takes up the most space?

Looking at your list of personal values, which matter most to you?

How do you spend your time at home at weekends?

Pie charts are also a great tool to investigate the truth of beliefs that can hold us back – as in Figure 10.3. For example, let's imagine Ahmed has depression, and thinks *'People won't like me unless I'm thin and attractive'* (thanks for that one, Instagram filters!). We could ask Ahmed to think of a friend or someone he really likes, and then tell us the qualities they have that he appreciates. For example, Ahmed might say he likes the fact his friend is:

- trusting

- fun

- kind

- reliable

- there for him

- attractive

- and has a sense of humour.

What Matters in a Friend

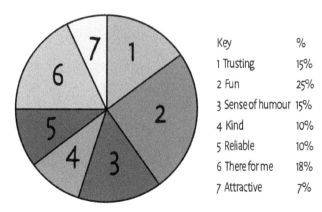

Key	%
1 Trusting	15%
2 Fun	25%
3 Sense of humour	15%
4 Kind	10%
5 Reliable	10%
6 There for me	18%
7 Attractive	7%

Figure 10.3: Pie charts are really useful devices for exploring beliefs and values

We'd then ask Ahmed to write a percentage for how important each quality is. After this, we could ask Ahmed to draw a circle and divide it up into slices of pizzas, each representing their size of importance.

We can then point out the graphic difference between the things Ahmed values in his friend and the things he values in himself. We could also wonder together if he has an unrealistic expectation of himself, and if it might be the depression talking rather than Ahmed's true values.

Continuum lines

Lines with '0' at one end and '10' at the other are a fairly common sight in low intensity work – but if you're not sick of the sight of them, 'continuum lines' are a way of exploring things when clients express things in terms of absolutes. For example, if a client says they feel anxious and like they're a scared person 100 per cent of the time, you could open this up. Write at the far left of a long line, 'scared 100 per cent', and at the right end of the line write 'safe and confident 100 per cent'. You can then look together at different times in the past week when the client might have felt slightly less anxious, and ask the client to write them on sticky notes and place them on the line. Continuum lines are a good way of doing Socratic dialogue in practice and can help a client deepen their understanding of their difficulty within the context of their lives, and also start to reassess their idea of the power the problem has over their lives.

Plants

It's not exactly evidence-based practice, but this is a rather lovely idea from Octavia Bell – a CAMHS clinical nurse specialist. At their second or third session, Octavia sometimes offers a small pot plant for the young person to look after. It can help imbue in a young person a sense of responsibility for caring for something, the therapeutic hope being that they may in time be able to transfer that sense of care onto themselves. You can also talk about the things a plant needs to survive and grow, and segue nicely into talking about what a young person might need. After all, water, sun and soil are the positive maintenance factors in a plant's growth – what's the equivalent for the young person?

TAKE-AWAYS

► Once we're really familiar with cognitive behavioural models, it's easier to start thinking about metaphorical ways of describing them based on the client's interests.

► There are lots of visual ways of working that clients can find more accessible and easier to understand than just talking.

► Analogies like bundles of string, train tracks, clean and messy cupboards can all be useful when thinking about different states of mind, and the way everyone's minds work differently.

CHAPTER 11

Safeguarding, Risk Assessment and Safety Planning

Risk and safeguarding need consideration throughout an intervention. During difficult conversations involving disclosures we have to keep calm and carry on – a bit like a swan…outwardly serene but paddling furiously under the surface. There are some ways of making it easier, though – including the way we raise questions. This entire chapter comes with a few big caveats. Follow your own organisation's safeguarding policies, stay within your role's remit, and think carefully about your skills development in this area with your supervisor.

THIS CHAPTER COVERS:

- The basics of safeguarding
- The practicalities of working with disclosures of suicidal thinking and self-harm
- Ideas on how to develop your risk assessment skills
- A simple idea for making a brief safety plan

WHAT IS SAFEGUARDING?

'Safeguarding' means playing our part in ensuring the safety of the young people we're working with. It's a constant part of the job, and you should receive a really thorough, robust training in safeguarding both at university and in your service. You should also be 100 per cent familiar with relevant safeguarding policies including those of any schools you're deployed in.

But no matter how much reading you do, and however familiar you are with the different types of abuse and different legal acts, I don't think any training gives an adequate sense of just how unclear and anxiety-making handling disclosures can be.

You have to quickly switch into a different 'mode' when a safeguarding concern arises and focus on following the relevant processes and procedures. Pilots have checklists and quickly turn to them when they encounter difficulties – we need to do the same. Having a clear plan of what to say when will help keep you a bit more clear-headed. Sometimes you might worry that passing on a concern might make life more difficult for a child, but it is never your job to hold a disclosure on your own. We don't keep secrets – which is why it's so important to explain the limits of confidentiality right at the start of our work.

TRY IT OUT: a safeguarding role play

You're working with a 12-year-old boy. He tells you that his Mum hits him on the head with a TV remote control when he fights with his sister. It's been going on for the past year. He says his Mum gets really upset when she's been drinking. Things got much worse when his Mum's partner left.

Remembering the swan metaphor, practise listening and staying calm while working out the next steps in your mind – and then tell your client what you think needs to happen next in order to ensure their safety.

After the role play, discuss how you found it with your colleague and any difficulties you had. Were you clear about what to do next? Using your own organisation's safeguarding policies, try to come up with an action plan as to how to handle safeguarding disclosures that you hear directly, or through a third party.

For nearly all practitioners the ground rule when working within schools is to always pass on safeguarding concerns to the school designated safeguarding lead yourself, verbally and in writing, on the same day. It is critically important that the school is informed that day. You should also tell your team and supervisor.

SUICIDAL THOUGHTS AND SELF-HARM

Due to the often-intimate relationship between mental health and self-harm and suicidal ideation, it's really important we ask about it. Of course – it is inevitably anxiety-provoking, and I wouldn't want to downplay just how difficult it can feel to raise these questions. On suicide awareness training courses, one of the big steps you're asked to take is to ask the facilitator, *'Have you ever had thoughts about killing yourself?'* It doesn't exactly trip off the tongue.

However, it's really important we can go there and ask just that. Suicide research experts have concluded that people who are struggling with suicidal thoughts usually welcome the openness in the enquiry (O'Connor, 2021). 'It is crucial we promote the conversation around suicide, so that more people will feel less alone and get the support and help they require,' writes Rory O'Connor, a man who has devoted his life to investigating the causes of suicide, and how we can best help those at risk (2021, p.11).

Meanwhile, remember the limits of your responsibilities with risk. EMHPs and CWPs are trained to assess and safety plan in response to risk, but not to work with current risks as part of interventions. That means that if a young person is continuing to self-harm or have active suicidal thoughts during an intervention, a low intensity practitioner will likely need to refer them on to a more specialist practitioner. And after any disclosure, you will need to consider with your supervisor whether ongoing treatment is appropriate within your role. You shouldn't be expected to ever 'hold' risk in the way a lead practitioner at CAMHS might.

ASKING ABOUT RISK

Some ways of asking about risk are easier than others. First, it's usually easier to ask about it in the context of the difficulty the client's seeking help with, rather than asking about it 'out of the blue'. Don't ask about risk as part of a check-box exercise in between questions about friendships and academic progress. Second, when it comes to asking the question, consider prefacing it by normalising suicidal thoughts and self-harm in the context of mental health difficulties: they're really common for young people struggling with anxiety or depression. Third, always empathise about how tough those difficulties can be, before finally asking if it's something they experience. Fourth, also consider modelling the fact you're okay with however they answer – as a mental health professional it's a question you ask lots.

Perhaps during an assessment you've been talking with a young person about their depression, and they tell you they don't see the point of anything any more. This is the moment to empathise with that difficulty, and also normalise it and enquire about risk. You might say something like, 'Wow, this sounds so hard for you. Some young people I've worked with who are really down have thoughts about wanting to end their life – that can happen with depression. Is that something you've ever experienced?'

If you're working with a young person who is telling you about how anxious they get, after exploring their anxiety further you could then segue into: 'This sounds awful for you. I know it's a difficult question to answer but I work with some young people who sometimes hurt themselves when they're feeling really anxious. Is that something you ever do?'

WHAT NEXT?

If a young person discloses suicidal thoughts or self-harm, then what next? If you're a new practitioner, be reassured that at first you'll simply be expected to empathise and tell the young person you'll need to talk to others about them to keep them safe.

You might want to practise this now, to feel more well-versed. You could say something like, 'Thanks so much for telling me this. My number one job is to help young people stay safe, so like we discussed in our first session, I think we should talk to your parent and the safeguarding officer about this. Is there a way you'd prefer me to do that? Should we ring them together?'

Or you might say, 'That sounds so difficult and something we can get extra help for you for. Lots of other people struggle with their emotions like this. Can we have a chat about the next steps?'

Again – these are just suggestions – it really is important you discuss the approach with your supervisor and follow your own team's policies.

TRY IT OUT: asking about self-harm and suicidal thoughts

Ask your supervisor if you can role play asking risk questions in a supervision session. It's so helpful to have a space to stumble about and find what phrases work best for you. Perhaps your supervisor can tell you what they'd say too, so you can see how it feels from the client's perspective.

I still find asking these questions uncomfortable. Some advice I was given by Sarah Goodfellow, the lead mental health nurse in my CAMHS team, was to try to feel your feet on the ground, and just try to stay in the moment of difficulty with the person you're with. It's a bit like standing next to a fast-flowing river – keep one foot firmly planted on the solid ground of the bank while you dip your other foot in the water. Over time, you get better at being able to keep thinking with a half-clear head even when your amygdala is going berserk. So – just be nice to yourself, take a breath and take it slowly.

If you have had previous experience in working with risk you might feel confident enough to ask some follow-up questions to develop the risk assessment further before then passing on your concerns – and we cover some of these in the next section. The main thing is to be honest with your supervisor about your level of experience and confidence around asking risk-related questions. They can then best support you and help you develop confidence. You should never feel alone when working with risk – always feel like you're part of a team.

Advanced skills: risk assessment tips

More experienced practitioners may feel confident enough to enquire further about risk and start safety planning in order to keep the young person safe in the short term. In this section, we look at how we can do this sensitively and skilfully, using some tips from some Specialist CAMHS duty and risk practitioners.

During a more advanced risk assessment it's important to ascertain levels of intent, planning and severity in order to understand what kind of help and support is going to be most needed. However, this can provoke a sense of undue pressure to dig out this information at all costs. While it's true that we do need to find out how much control a young person has over their thoughts and actions, and whether they have any active intent or plan to end their lives, a more exploratory approach is generally more comfortable for a young person and can lead to a fuller picture.

Emily Blake, lead practitioner at a CAMHS duty and risk team, advises that a good risk assessment is '70 per cent about the function of the suicidal thoughts or self-harm, and 30 per cent about the nuts and bolts of what they've done or might do.'

Emily continues; 'I like to ask the "why" before the "how". For example, if they tell me they feel really low and rubbish all the time, I'll be curious about what happens those times just before they self-harm or feel suicidal. What's triggering it? Are there arguments at home, or maybe stresses about homework, or friendship issues happening?'

After the 'why', you can find out what they do when they feel that way. Do they act on the thoughts, and if so, are they acting protectively or dangerously? Are there times they manage to not self-harm, by distracting themselves, for example? Understanding this helps us work on safety together. If they're already taking protective steps (e.g. sterilising the sharp object), we can think about how to build on these strengths. If they're acting dangerously (for example, walking off towards a high bridge they have their mind on), we could start making some suggestions as to what they could try to do differently.

After thinking about the function, we can next ask about the important basics. What methods do they use if self-harming?

How do they feel during and after it? Do they know about safe and unsafe self-harm? If suicidal, have they made plans? How many times have they prepared in some way – for example, writing a note, or giving stuff away, or stockpiling substances, or taking a bus somewhere to check out a plan?

'If someone is both suicidal and self-harming, it's good to learn more about the function of self-harm and if it makes them feel more or less suicidal,' says Emily. 'Sometimes a sense of shame around self-harm can increase suicidality, other times it can act as a release and decrease it.'

Being curious with a young person about what's going on for them is something they might not have experienced before. Revelations of self-harm or suicidality can lead to strong and sometimes panicked reactions from adults. This is why we need to try to avoid running through a list of triggering questions.

'The young person might have never joined the dots and seen there's a link between when Dad gets really cross and they want to end it all, or that the thoughts are there all the time,' says Emily. 'When done well, these kinds of conversations help extend a client's capacity to think through what's going on for them.'

If a young person is self-harming, you'll need to let them know that you'll need to talk to their parents or carers about removing sharp objects or access to medication (or whatever it is they're accessing or doing that's making them unsafe). We can remind them that our number one priority is to keep young people safe, and we all sometimes need help from others in managing difficult urges and impulses. As research shows (Berry, Law and Ryan, 2021), it really matters to young people that professionals are honest and transparent about any communications with parents.

Finally, write up a safety plan with the young person or parent so there's a document showing that the next steps have been thought about and agreed. The main aim is to ensure the young person can keep themselves safe in the short term.

A very simple form of safety planning (see Table 11.1) includes running through the following five questions with a client, and writing down the answers as thoroughly as possible:

1. What are you doing or experiencing that poses some risk?

2. What makes it safe, or a bit safer?

3. What would make it more risky or dangerous?

4. What steps do you agree to take to keep safe?

5. When and who will review this plan?

Advanced skills: talking about self-harm with parents

As we get more familiar with working with self-harm disclosures, it can be easy to forget just what a shock it might be for a parent to learn their child has self-harmed, and also just how big a step it is for a child to tell us.

Jaki Watkins, a senior schools wellbeing practitioner, advises us to never forget the role of shame and guilt in mental health and to hold these in mind when talking with parents.

'Often young people won't want their parents to know about their self-harm, because they'll fear their reaction – whether that's tears, or anger or an over-intrusion as they see it,' Jaki says. 'The young person might feel guilty about upsetting their parents or letting them down, or fear around them starting to monitor them 24/7, or perhaps some shame around having self-harmed. Equally, parents might feel guilt or shame around their child's wellbeing.'

We can help a parent by normalising, validating and empathising, for example:

'I know this must be difficult to hear, but it's important for you to know as their parent...'

'You're definitely not alone in this...a lot of young people who are having a hard time with their wellbeing can self-harm, as unfortunately the statistics show...'

'It's totally normal to have strong feelings as a parent about this, and you might need some time for it to sink in, but then it'd be great to talk together about how we can work together to help your young person with this in the best way possible...'

Perhaps you could practise these kinds of conversations with colleagues, too.

Table 11.1: A simple safety plan

My Simple Safety Plan
What I'm doing or experiencing that's risky to my health is...
What makes it safe, or a bit safer, is...
What would make it more risky or dangerous is...
The steps I agree to taking to keep safe are...
Who's going to review this plan to check it's going okay, and when?

THE FIVE P'S

When writing up a risk assessment, many Specialist CAMHS services use the 'Five P's' as a way of thinking through and recording the risk.

You can use these as subheadings in your notes or merge it all into one paragraph – it doesn't matter, as long as all the factors are included. The Five P's are:

1. The Presenting risk – what's happening or happened

2. Predisposing – the factors that mean a child is more vulnerable to risk

3. Precipitating – the stressors, triggers or other developmental factors

4. Perpetuating – factors that are maintaining the likelihood of it happening

5. Protective – the things that keep the person safe.

Asking ourselves these questions when we're writing up our notes can help us sort through the information we've been given and write up a risk formulation. It can also serve as a prompt for us to make a follow-up call to find out more information, if needed.

TAKE-AWAYS

▶ Safeguarding is everyone's responsibility, including ours.

▶ We need to ask directly about risk and it's a skill we can practise to get more comfortable with.

▶ Asking about risk in the context of the presenting mental health difficulty is less jarring than asking about it out of context.

▶ It's normal to have a raised heartrate when hearing a disclosure – we need to remain calm and professional and just take things slowly, step by step.

▶ Always pass safeguarding concerns to the school-designated lead on the same day.

▶ More experienced practitioners may wish to develop further skills in risk assessment and safety planning, but it is never a CWP's or EMHP's job to hold risk.

CHAPTER 12

How to Make an Onward Referral

Sometimes something crops up that's beyond a CWP's or EMHP's remit. You might have picked up on compulsive behaviours and be wondering about OCD, or perhaps you're concerned about restricted eating habits – or a young person tells you they're suffering loads of nightmares and flashbacks from a traumatic event. In these situations, it's important to know how to make an onward referral so your client can access appropriate support.

THIS CHAPTER COVERS:

- How to manage this kind of situation in a session
- How 'thresholds' affect what services can offer
- The components of a good onward referral letter

RECOGNISING THE ISSUE

It should go without saying that if you're considering an onward referral, you'll need discuss it in supervision and with colleagues. But it's also important to know how to raise the idea of 'referring on' when you're in a session with a young person.

First of course it's important to acknowledge the difficulty with the young person. For example, you could validate with 'This difficulty sounds really hard...'.

The next step may well be familiar to you from Chapter 5 – when we have to consider 'signposting' on to other services. One way of doing that might be to say, 'This difficulty might be something that a more specialist service might be able to really help you with. Can I tell you more about it? It's just an idea and I'd have to check it out further with my team, but I'd really like to hear your thoughts on it.'

Within the session it might also be important to think together with the young person about what resources are going to help them in the short term. You might ask questions like:

'What helps you cope right now?'

'What strengths do you have?'

'Who else could you talk to about this difficulty to help you feel supported?'

With a younger child, you could do the 'five fingers of support' exercise: get them to put their hand on a paper and draw around it, while asking them to write down people in their life they could reach out to in the meantime. If they can't think of five, you can always help them by asking about wider friends and family, school staff, and suggesting apps and phone and text services.

Remembering how important reliability is (Ryan *et al.*, 2021), agree a time when you'll come back to them with an update. It may take a week or more for you to talk with your supervisor or their parent, or have a consultation with the service you're thinking of referring to, so be sure to manage expectations.

WHERE TO REFER TO?

Senior practitioners within an MHST or CWP service may be able to offer interventions for more complex moderate mental health difficulties, and of course it's worth knowing about if this is the case, and how it works. It's also worth getting familiar with the specialist services available both locally and nationally and understanding their referral criteria – what kind of cases they take on and what they offer.

When talking about referrals, lots of professionals talk about 'thresholds'. These are the degrees of complexity or difficulty at which a service will accept a referral. So – most MHSTs will have a low threshold, just needing to see evidence of mild to moderate problems, but ongoing self-harm may well be 'above their threshold'. Equally, the national eating disorder charity BEAT has a low threshold and provides advice to all parents. At the opposite end of the scale, many NHS eating disorder services have extremely high thresholds. Some only accept referrals for young people when their difficulty is becoming life-threatening.

HOW TO WRITE AN EFFECTIVE ONWARD REFERRAL

Whether you submit a referral through an online portal or by letter or email, try to avoid overly emotive language and stick to the facts. It's much more likely to be successful if you can include some really key information:

- a 5WFIDO type assessment of the difficulty which details the chronicity, severity and history of the problem

- any contributory factors

- any current risk, or risk factors (a Five P's is ideal)

- any routine outcome measures, such as RCADS

- detail the degree of the CYP's current functioning

- outline the help provided so far and the CYP's responsiveness to that help.

It's always useful to discuss the referral with a practitioner over the phone, if possible, and this may help your referral's chances of being accepted too.

An example referral letter

Dear Specialist CAMHS,

Following a consultation call with your duty worker this morning, I'd be grateful if you'd consider Tegan Rush, a 14-year-old young person who identifies as female, for assessment and treatment for anxiety and possibly assessment for ASC (autistic spectrum condition) within your specialist service.

Presentation and work so far

I have worked with Tegan for eight sessions of low intensity CBT, using graded exposure, but this has failed to help. I am including a summary of Outcome Measures to date. Tegan reports feeling anxious most days for several hours a day. The anxiety has got considerably worse in the last 12 months and in discussions with my supervisor we agree they'd benefit from more specialist assessment.

Risk

Tegan has self-harmed by scratching for the past 12 months and in the past two months she has also been cutting her forearms using sharp objects. Her parents are aware. Tegan is able to talk to them and they have taken necessary safety steps to remove sharps as per our safety plan. However, last week Tegan started using a broken piece of glass and seems insistent on continuing. Tegan has also expressed some suicidal ideation and says she suffers distressing suicidal thoughts daily. She has not expressed intent or plan to any adults as far as I am aware.

Functioning

Tegan stopped attending school in October and has a total average of 10 per cent attendance for this academic year. She has also stopped seeing her friends and no longer goes to her weekly sports club. Indeed, she rarely leaves the house, avoids shops and spends most of her time in her bedroom.

Parents report that Tegan's appetite is reduced to one meal a day, and that she has a disrupted sleep pattern with only four to five hours of sleep per night.

School and parents all share concerns that Tegan's presentation and functioning is decreasing, with the severity of anxiety increasing.

Systemic factors

Tegan lives with her Mum and younger sister. Mum has been responsive to our MHST's suggestions and engaged with trying to reduce reassurance and follow steps as per our plans, however this has not proved successful. She sees her Dad on alternate weekends but there is no variation in her presentation in each home, according to parents. There is no current social service involvement.

Please let me know the outcome of your decision regarding this referral. Thanks!

Best wishes,
Finn

TAKE-AWAYS

▶ If you think a young person needs additional support, acknowledge the difficulty and then think with them about what might be helpful next.

▶ It's important to consider any gaps in support. Help a young person reflect on their currently available resources.

▶ Thresholds are the levels of difficulty at which services will be able to offer an intervention, based on factors including commissioning and their expertise.

▶ A referral checklist can help to ensure you pass on all relevant information.

CHAPTER 13

Self-Reflective Practice and Supervision

Facilitating a session can feel a bit like driving on a busy motorway at 70 mph at night while trying to read the sat nav and listen to your friend's life story all at once. Doing the double – staying alongside your client while sticking to the session protocol – can be both intense and tiring. Self-reflective practice and supervision are valuable breathing spaces which help us look after ourselves, stay on track and develop our evolving craftsmanship.

THIS CHAPTER COVERS:

- How to develop self-reflective skills
- The difference between 'case management' and 'clinical' supervision
- How supervisors and supervisees can make supervision even better
- Tips from trainees on how to use group supervision

SELF-REFLECTIVE PRACTICE

One thing I really value about working in CAMHS is the chance for quick catch-ups with colleagues. If you're based in a clinical setting then after a session you can go back into the shared office, have a natter with a colleague and start to decompress. But when you're out in the wilds of the community – whether that's in a school, youth building or just working remotely from home – it's easy to feel a little lonesome with no one to 'offload' to.

This is where self-reflective practice can really help. It's about stepping back, reviewing and processing a session. Ideally, it'll help you be more objective and not take things too personally when things don't go so well. Think of the process as being about 'creating a bit more loft space', or developing your own 'internal supervisor'.

One team of EMHPs came up with the following list of questions that they find useful to ask themselves after a session. You might just pick two or three that jump out at you each time. They're not meant for self-assessing your competencies – rather to create some space so it's easier to be reflective. At best, asking yourself these questions will help you tease out the things you can be proud of and things you'd like to change next time.

Self-reflective questions checklist
In general...

Was I prepared enough?

What went well?

How closely did I follow the session guidelines?

When I went off-track, why did I do so, and how did it work out?

Are there any safeguarding concerns I need to share or talk through today?

Any feelings...

What am I feeling after that session?

How did the client feel in that session?

Was I being judgemental about anything?

Did any other factors in my life affect how I felt?

Is this bringing up anything for me personally I need to think more about?

Summing up…

What was really effective in the session?

What could I do differently next time?

Do I need to take anything to supervision?

Any risk issues I need to discuss or raise?

TRY IT OUT: self-reflective practice

You'll probably need to lock yourself away in a cupboard or the school staff toilets to do this, but try to carve yourself out ten minutes with a cup of tea after your next few sessions to answer some of the above questions. It should help you 'close' each session – see if it means you feel more fresh and ready for your next client.

SUPERVISION

A good supervisor will support, teach, encourage and challenge you. Clinical psychologist Duncan Law (2021) states that the ultimate purpose of supervision is to improve both the supervisee's practice and the outcome of their intervention. A good supervisor will always have one eye out for how their supervisee's practice will positively affect the young person, because that is our ultimate goal.

Supervision should include discussion, role plays, teaching, reflection, brainstorming, conceptualising, risk management and much more – it should be a really rich, varied experience. A good supervisor will be self-assessing themselves using a competencies model (SAGE is a commonly used one) and working hard to improve their own practice, just as all good EMHPs or CWPs do too.

Most importantly, a good supervisor will make their supervisee feel comfortable and able to bring all their mistakes and mess-ups to supervision. Of course, it can be tempting to only talk about the good stuff. A supervisor should make sure supervisees bring all of their cases and not just the ones they want to show off. A non-judgemental space allows practitioners to raise the cases that are most needing supervision input – for example, when there are sudden drops in outcome measures – so they can problem solve together in the best interests of the young person.

A quick word about two different types of supervision. There's 'clinical supervision' and 'case management'. Clinical supervision is about helping you with your cases and supporting you with them. Case management is more about helping you manage your overall case load, and it might also involve 'job planning' – organising the structure of your working day. Quite often, both of these activities will take place with the same supervisor. What might make it more confusing is if your supervisor is also your line manager. Then they have responsibility for you as an employee, and that stuff around managing your 'performance' creeps in. A good supervisor will work with you to demarcate each of these three roles, so one doesn't encroach on or blur into the other.

In terms of clinical supervision, good supervisors will structure a session much like you would one of your own sessions. You'll set an agenda together, discuss cases, perhaps do a role play, think about safeguarding and referrals, and assess at the end how useful it's all been – perhaps using the helpful aspects of supervision questionnaire (HASQ) form. At times your supervisor might interrupt you to try to keep you on track – there should be clear time management and expectations set so you get the absolute best out of the session.

Be mindful that EMHP and CWP supervisors often come from a diverse range of training backgrounds, including art therapy, psychodynamic counselling and clinical psychology, so will have varying degrees of knowledge and familiarity with low intensity CBT. In fact, you may well be far more familiar with the manuals or protocols than your supervisor. That's okay. A good supervisor will acknowledge any gaps in their understanding. This shouldn't come between you as an issue. And through their own supervisor training, they will be learning more about CBT and how 'adherence to the model' is so important within the low intensity practitioner role. Quite often a shift in understanding occurs, particularly for those coming from a psychodynamic orientation, where supervisors have to make a big switch from being mainly 'process-orientated' to being more 'content-orientated'. What I mean by this is that much of the focus in psychodynamic work is thinking about the dynamics in the therapeutic relationship which psychodynamic theory posits facilitates the process of change. With low intensity work reviewing the working alliance is essential, too, but we focus a lot more on the content – it's a more 'how did it go compared with the session plan' kind of approach.

To make the most of supervision, come prepared with one or two specific questions you'd like help with. For example: 'I did an exposure ladder with Asimah but she was really sceptical about it and I felt like I was being pushy. Can we discuss what I did and different ways I could approach this next time with a kid who just doesn't get it?'

Just as in low intensity CBT, supervision should be goal-based, so after each session you'll both be able to judge how useful it's been. Did you get out of it what you wanted? What could be done better next time? How would you measure your competency in a particular skill, and what's the plan as you work to improve it?

GROUP SUPERVISION AND VIDEO CLIPS

Most university courses include group supervision or practice tutor groups. But who'd want to ever show a video of themselves at work to other people? It's so cringe-making! But sharing videos is actually a great way to experience graded exposure. You'll have to go through it to believe it. Not that I'm one to talk. I found it so hard to show videos of myself floundering. I only really liked to show good moments, which while nice for my ego, wasn't exactly helping me develop as a practitioner – but it was so useful to hear others' views of what I could do differently when I eventually found the courage to show myself struggling.

In terms of giving feedback to others, here are some thoughts from a team of low-intensity practitioners on what they find most helpful:

'Sometimes it's more effective for the person who's shown the clip to give their thoughts first.'

'Reassurance and empathy from others can be so helpful if you're sharing a difficult case you're struggling with.'

'Hearing someone repeat back what I did means I sometimes recognise some of the stuff that I've done as being good, for the first time ever, as I haven't recognised it myself.'

'If someone can model something to me and act it out, it's so much more helpful than saying it. So rather than saying "you could have been more empathic", show me how I could have been – what I could have said differently and so on.'

TAKE-AWAYS

▶ Doing self-reflective practice is like building an extension in a home: it gives you a bit of extra space to process each session in a constructive way.

▶ Good supervision should support and encourage you and help you develop as a practitioner.

▶ Just like any good session, supervision should involve agenda setting and giving feedback.

▶ To make the most of it, come prepared with specific questions.

▶ Showing videos and getting feedback in group supervision can seem daunting but most practitioners find it really valuable. Having others 'show' rather than 'tell' is particularly useful.

Part 3

TIPS FOR INTERVENTIONS

■ CHAPTER 14 ■

The Value of Compassion

Compassion-focused therapy is one of a new 'third wave' of therapies that has an encouraging emerging evidence base. The reason for integrating some compassion-focused practices into our work is simple: we're often our harshest critics, and clients are often their worst critics, too. So, before we delve into some of the core components of effective low intensity work, let's stop and think about how we can develop a little more kindness and compassion towards ourselves and help our clients do the same.

> ### THIS CHAPTER COVERS:
>
> • Why self-compassion matters
> • Some ideas as to how to integrate self-compassion for ourselves and clients

Just as nearly all psychological theories would suggest, I'm sure you and I have both been shaped to some degree by how we were treated – both good and bad – early on in life. And we're not alone! I recently attended a workshop run by psychologist David Trickey, one of the UK's top child trauma experts. Now it's normal in workshops to get to see the expert in action, but David apologised and said he wouldn't be showing any demo video of himself at work. He said he'd tried to record sessions with actors but kept either freezing or becoming a bumbling mess! David generously shared that he knew the problem stemmed from a fear of not coming across well. He revealed how his own inner critic relentlessly drove him on to try harder, do more therapy, be better and better. These things run deep!

I'd imagine at times you're not your kindest critic either. And in this work our attitude to ourselves really matters. We need to learn to forgive ourselves for the things that don't go as planned – inevitable when working in schools. We could try to like ourselves as the fallible human beings we are, instead of berating ourselves for not being the practitioners we'd like to be. Life is no fun when self-criticism wins, and when we can't empathise and care for ourselves it's also harder to empathise and care for others (Gilbert, 2009). As practitioners we need to master some of these skills and convey compassion so we can also help our clients activate their own inner supportive voice (Carona et al., 2017). It's like those safety instructions on the plane – learn how to get the oxygen mask of compassion on yourself before you help your fellow passenger get theirs on.

So – it's worth exploring compassion and its value in our work in more depth. Thankfully, psychologists like Paul Gilbert, Kristen Neff and Christ Germer have done just that and researched why compassion matters and how it can be integrated into practice. Paul Gilbert (2009) describes compassion as a sensitivity to the suffering and distress in ourselves and others and a commitment to help alleviate it. One of the big levers in compassion-focused therapy is activating our internal soothing system – switching on the caring, parenting side of ourselves, and applying the care we might give our nearest and dearest to ourselves as well. Without these instincts, our species wouldn't have survived.

As Germer (2009) suggests, being able to be kind to ourselves when we're experiencing emotional discomfort is far healthier than being harshly critically to ourselves for having that discomfort. This is especially true with anxiety (see Chapter 18). It's a case of saying to ourselves, 'Even as I feel as I do, how can I be kind to myself?' Lots of studies have suggested that a compassionate approach is more helpful. If you're a university student, being able to be compassionate to yourself increases your ability to cope with academic set-backs (Neff and Dahm, 2015) and there's good emerging evidence for the effectiveness of compassion-focused therapy with many emotional wellbeing difficulties (Kirby, 2016).

Here are a few taster ideas as to how to include some self-compassion in practical ways in your work to benefit clients. You might also want to try them out for yourself.

TWO TEACHERS

Russell Kolts suggests that the reason many of us engage in self-criticism is to 'attempt to motivate, protect or keep ourselves in line' (2016, p.110). If we suspect that our client is strongly self-critical, then the Two Teachers vignette is worth exploring with them. Developed by Paul Gilbert (2009), it's a way of exploring whether listening to self-criticism is always useful, and what it'd be like to shift to a more self-compassionate approach.

An exercise

Imagine you have a five-year-old cousin called Ethan who you're really fond of. At his primary school he's got two teachers: one works Mondays and Tuesdays the other Wednesdays through Fridays. Your cousin finds it hard to sit still at circle time and the first teacher gets really cross with him and tells him in front of all his friends that he's a fidget bum and needs to learn to sit still. At the end of breaktime, she gets impatient and shouts at him when he doesn't listen to the whistle and keeps playing. When he can't think of an answer to a question in class, she says, 'What's wrong with you?' She's pretty harsh and tries to motivate him by running him down.

His second teacher is calmer and more patient. He really wants his children to learn and understands that sitting still is really hard for some young kids. When your cousin can't sit still, his second teacher quietly goes over to him and passes him a fidget toy. In breaktime, he says, 'Hey you've got loads of energy, how about dribbling a football as fast as you can to the end of the playground and back and see if you can make it before I blow my whistle!' When your cousin can't think of an answer to a question in class, the teacher says, 'I can see you tried to think really hard there – good job for trying – it's not easy this!'

So – a few questions. Which teacher would you prefer for your cousin who you really care about? Why is that? Which do you think would do a better job of teaching Ethan? What's the difference? And when you yourself are struggling, which teacher does the voice in your head sound like? Which voice would you prefer to have?

As Kolts says, this exercise should help our client *feel* the difference in the approaches, rather than just *cognitively acknowledge* the difference. By helping the client feel it, the hope is they will connect with a realisation that being kinder to yourself – more of an encouraging coach than a belittling bully – is not only a nicer experience, but also more productive in helping us get to wherever we want to go.

A LETTER TO YOURSELF

Letter writing is a way of connecting your compassionate side with difficult experiences. Kristen Neff (2011) suggests that many of us find it easier to show kindness to a friend or family member than we do ourselves. We can ask our client to write a letter from the perspective of a friend or loved one – someone really kind. It could even be a fictional figure – a character from a movie perhaps. By putting themselves in someone else's shoes, they might find it easier to find compassion for themselves. It's a way of side-stepping our own inner critic for a moment. We then try to build a bridge between the client's sense of compassion and a difficulty they are experiencing in their lives.

For example, if a parent is really struggling with their child's difficult behaviour, we could ask them to think of the kindest person they know and imagine what this kind person might say to them as they struggle at home when their child is kicking off. What would they say about what they know and like about them? About how all parents struggle at times? About how they are doing the best they can? What advice would they give them?

If a teenager is struggling with anxiety, we could invite them to do something really relaxing so they feel nice and calm, and then ask them to think of a time they felt really anxious. Keeping their anxious self in mind, we could ask them to write a letter of support, telling them they understand how terrible they feel, and letting them know that it's so common for people to feel this way, and that they accept and like them even more for having the courage to try to deal with this anxiety.

For yourself, well maybe at times you just think you're doing the worst job ever and are no good at all at it – welcome to the club if you do! Perhaps you could write a letter now to yourself, imagining a time in the future when you might struggle. You might want to remind yourself of the values that brought you into this work, and the qualities and competencies you are aiming to develop along the way. You could point out that it would be unusual not to have a moment of doubt in your abilities, and you are just another member of the human race for feeling this way. Maybe you could even encourage yourself to have a cup of tea.

TRY IT OUT: a letter to your future self

Write yourself a letter to your future self, reminding your future self of the values you hold dear that have brought you into this line of work. Remind them what you want for them in life, and what matters. Tell them what you'd like them to do for themselves if they ever feel stressed or burnt out. Look up self-compassion.org for full guidance on self-compassion letter writing.

THREE GOOD THINGS

For clients who aren't well practised in noticing and savouring the good moments in life, this is a great exercise. The 'three good things in life' daily practice was first developed by Seligman *et al.* (2005) and has some good evidence behind it (Lee, 2017). Ask your client to think of three things they've appreciated during the day – something they've been proud of, felt grateful for or that has made them smile. They can record them each evening by paper or pen, or by making a quick selfie video. Why does it work? Well, as Beaumont and Welford (2020) put it, we're programmed to pay more attention to threats during the day rather than positive things, so this is a great way of rebalancing things. By consciously trying to recall three positive things each evening – even if they're simple things (like 'a shopkeeper smiled, Mum didn't shout and I got to school on time') – we're turning up the volume on the positives, and learning to spot and appreciate kindness in our daily life. There are also some great apps for this activity – 'Delightful' is one.

MINDFUL SELF-COMPASSION

There are lots of practical things we can do to be kind to ourselves – whether that's spending more time with friends, going for a walk, having a hot chocolate instead of a coffee, or just spending an extra minute in a nice warm shower. There are also excellent self-compassion mindfulness exercises available online. Chris Germer (2009) writes that the very act of accepting how we feel and what we think requires a fair amount of self-compassion, but this part of the puzzle is often not acknowledged in western mindfulness practice. A self-compassion mindfulness exercise will lead you through acknowledging any difficult feelings and thoughts, accepting them and recognising the common humanity in the experience, and then consciously trying to bring some kindness to your experience – not in the hope of changing it, but just because you deserve that kindness.

TAKE-AWAYS

► Trying to be more compassionate to ourselves can help us be more effective practitioners.

► Practical ways of helping clients develop self-compassion include helping clients notice and appreciate the good things in life and helping them develop a kinder 'inner coach'.

► Encouraging clients to practise good self-care including mindfulness exercises is another way of putting self-compassion into practice.

CHAPTER 15

The Importance of Back-Up Teams

'It's not all on you' – that's such an important message for young people and parents to hear. Helping someone think about their network of support – which can include family members, friends, school staff or other key people – can reduce any sense of aloneness in their struggle and increase the support they feel in achieving their goals.

THIS CHAPTER COVERS:

- Creative ways of helping a client identify their network of support known as 'back-up teams'
- Why it's useful to review a back-up team once in a while during the intervention

---

As the poet John Donne said, 'no man is an island entirely unto himself'. Helping someone identify their network of support can help reveal the way they see their place in things and who really matters to them. A good back-up team exercise helps reveal who our client can lean on in times of need and also how connected and supported they feel by those around them.

This is useful information in many ways. Most importantly, having access to social support in times of difficulty or even crisis is a 'moderating factor' in reducing the emotional impact of such difficulties, as O'Connor (2021) puts it. Doing a back-up team exercise can help a young person identify who they would feel most comfortable turning to for support – and we can then help them work out when and how they could do just that, and what might get in the way (for example, by problem solving and doing role plays).

This is so important. When people go through extreme emotional distress they often feel they're a burden to others and also feel entrapped by their difficulties. Researchers have concluded that these are two key common factors that make it really hard for them to reach out for help (O'Connor, 2021).

Whether facing a crisis or not, social support is usually essential for clients when they're engaging in the hard graft of making changes and working towards their goals. One session per week from us is a tiny amount of support compared with the difference good friends, school staff and family can make. As a personal example, there's no way I'd have finished this book without all the contributions from illustrators, editors and practitioners, without the help of friends checking chapters or my partner helping me switch off in the evening. To get a quick sense of this for yourself, have a think about the people in your life who are supporting you as you do your training, or really helped you get through a difficulty recently – try mapping them out using one of the exercises below.

And from what we know about the teenage brain, it is even more important for adolescents to have this network in place. With the amygdala firing on all four cylinders but the rational, reasoning, 'whoa, hold on there, let's just have a think about this' pre-frontal cortex still undergoing major reconstruction (Monk *et al.*, 2003), teenagers can really benefit from the help of those around them to regulate their emotions and make changes. Roslyn Law (2021) describes this as 'borrowing pre-frontal cortex capacity'. Getting others involved is like plugging an external hard drive into your laptop to extend its storage capacity.

There're a few creative ways we can wonder with a young person, child or parent about who they value in their life and who might be able to be a source of support, comfort and even challenge as they work towards their goals. Here are some ideas.

SOCIAL CIRCLES

'Social circles' (see Figure 15.1 on the next page) is an idea from interpersonal psychotherapy that's made its way into a broad range of practitioners' toolboxes. It's a simple, visual way of mapping out a support network. This is roughly how it goes:

> 'I'm really interested in your life and who matters the most to you. Would it be okay to ask more about them? If so, let's draw two circles like this, and while I'm doing that, can you think of all the people in your life you feel closest to?'

> 'Okay, could you drop a small stick person picture of yourself in the middle – or put a dot for yourself there?'

> 'Next can you write the names of the people in your life down, putting those you feel closest to you right in close to you, and those who you feel less close to further away?'

> 'Are there any other family members you could put down some-where? Any other friends? Any school staff, or other adults or people?'

You might also ask the client to underline anyone they think they could talk to about their difficulty, or who could be helpful. And it's fine if this includes pets. Mine definitely does.

The next stage is to ask your client, 'Out of these people, who do you think would be most helpful to you as you work towards your goal?'

You could ask the client to highlight or underline the people they want in their back-up team. It's then important to get specific and operationalise the plan, by asking for example:

> 'How could they be helpful – what sort of support will they offer?'

> 'When will you talk to them about it?'

> 'How will we know if it's been useful having them on the team?'

Some clients might feel awkward about asking their friend, family member or teacher for help. It might be helpful to role play the con-versation with them.

You may also want to ask about the people in the client's life who are not helpful or supportive. This can help normalise the fact that not everyone wants to ask close family members for support.

Of course, relationships change and it's good practice to review a client's back-up team as the intervention progresses. When new problems or difficulties emerge then that's also a good time to review the back-up team to think about any changes in their network and ongoing support.

▦ TRY IT OUT: your own social circles

Draw out your own social circles diagram, following the guidance in this chapter. Then put the diagram away and do another in four weeks' time. Then review the two diagrams together, to see any changes.

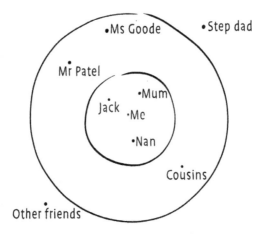

Figure 15.1: The classic 'social circles' exercise

TEAMS AND CREWS

There are endless ways of thinking about support networks that work from your client's own interests. If your client is in a football team, for example, perhaps you could draw out that and get them to write the names of the people close to them as the defenders, midfielders, attackers and goalkeeper. If a younger child is really into space and rockets, you could draw a spaceship (see Figure 15.2) and ask them who they'd like in their crew to accompany them on their mission to beat their anxiety.

At the time of writing, games like Minecraft® and Clash of Clans are popular. You could ask the young person what they're into, and who they'd place on their Minecraft® island or in their clan.

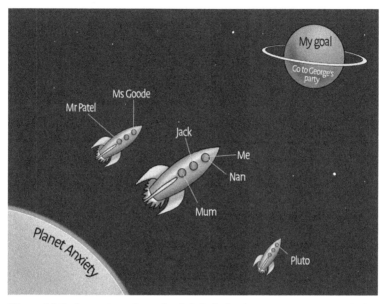

Figure 15.2: A creative take on 'social circles' using astronauts on a mission

DEVELOPMENTAL CONSIDERATIONS

Whichever way you do it, it's quite common for younger kids to put one or two family members right in close to them. With adolescents that's rarer – it's usually their friends. A key part of adolescent development is finding your own identity (often in opposition to others in the family). So, while younger primary school-aged children tend to listen to parents the most, then teachers, and last their friends – with teenagers it's the other way round. This can make it hard for teenagers to ask parents for support. So, we need to work extra hard to support parents in understanding their young people's difficulties and their need for space, but also the ways they can still support them and be alongside them.

I just told a joke to my 15-year-old son who's just come home from school. He looked at me a little strangely and said, 'You remind me a bit of my English teacher Mr Warren', then went upstairs. Dad jokes are just one of the casualties of adolescent individuation.

THINKING SYSTEMICALLY

As practitioners we can really help young people by supporting their network too – encouraging parents to attend some of the sessions and helping to ensure they become active 'co-therapists' where this is appropriate. Of course, there are many implications to this involvement and older teenagers are more likely to resist the involvement of parents. This needs to be respected. It's more about thinking of who can best serve as allies as we work to help our young person. This might lead us to want to arrange or attend 'team around the child' meetings where we support other professionals by adding our perspective to difficulties and give suggestions that dovetail with the interventions we offer. One really important aspect is psychoeducation – if key adults can really understand the 'method behind the madness' of trying to do things differently and crack those maintenance cycles then we'll be so much more likely to succeed. There's lots on this in Chapter 19 around working with parents of younger children – but it's equally important with adolescents. Again, always seek to take the young person's lead – ask them first if it's okay for you to talk to other adults, explain why you think it'd be helpful for them, and encourage them to be honest with you if it's not something they want you to do.

TAKE-AWAYS

▶ Helping a client reflect on who matters in their life will help increase their likelihood of using others to support them in their goals.

▶ There are loads of different creative ways of wondering about this with them, including social circles, spaceships and football teams.

▶ A client's back-up team can be reviewed as an intervention progresses – particularly useful if new difficulties emerge.

▶ If a young person agrees it would be useful, try to involve parents and school staff – skill them up with psychoeducation and get them alongside you and your client as they work towards their goals.

CHAPTER 16

How to Help with Sleep Hygiene

Don't forget the simple stuff – sleep, diet, exercise and so on – and how much this can impact young people. This chapter focuses on how we can help young people develop healthier sleep habits and help raise awareness around the increasingly solid links between sleep hygiene and good mental health.

THIS CHAPTER COVERS:

- The correlation between sleep and wellbeing
- Some interesting psychoeducation facts about sleep
- The steps we can help young people take to improve their sleep

---

SLEEP AND WELLBEING

Sleep allows our bodies and minds to recuperate so we can wake up refreshed and ready to go. It's an active thing: your brain is busy sorting through memories and filing things away in the right places at night – a bit like one of those PC cleaner apps – helping you to consolidate what you've learnt ready for the next day.

'It's important to remember that staying up late is usually counter-productive, even if you're cramming in revision,' says supervisor Jo Lamprinopoulou. 'Your brain has less time to process what it's learnt, you'll wake up more tired and you'll be less able to learn the next day.'

Of course, poor sleep doesn't just make studying less effective. Recent research points towards a correlation between reduced sleep and increased levels of mental health difficulty. A recent study showed that on average teenagers sleep for just six and a half hours per night – this is well below the recommended eight to nine hours. Just one hour of extra sleep makes a huge difference in terms of feeling hopeful and positive. Indeed, young people who lost those precious 60 minutes of sleep were at heightened risk of increased suicidal ideation and substance misuse (Winsler *et al.*, 2015).

But does poor sleep lead to poor mental health, or do mental health difficulties lead to poor sleep? Some studies indicate that poor sleep at 15 is correlated with anxiety and depression later in life (Orchard *et al.*, 2020), thus highlighting the importance of early interventions for sleep hygiene.

Psychiatrist David Veale (2021) suggests that there's a very circular relationship between mental health and sleep. It's not always easy to know which causes the other, but there's a causal link between the two. For example, we know that nine out of ten depressed teenagers have poor sleep (Goodyer *et al.*, 2017). And conversely, we know that teenagers who attend sleep clinics are at increased risk of depression (Inkelis *et al.*, 2021).

We can safely conclude that if we get a good night's sleep, it is highly likely to help us with our main mental health difficulty given the positive effects sleep has in keeping us emotionally regulated.

The following facts might be useful when talking about sleep with young people and parents and carers.

LACK OF SLEEP SETS THE AMYGDALA ON FIRE!

Researchers have found that when we're sleep-deprived, our amygdala is 60 per cent more emotionally reactive (Walker, 2018). The amygdala – as we discuss in Chapter 18 – is the part of our brain that's involved in our fight, flight, freeze response. When we sleep well, our brains are more balanced and more able to keep us on an even keel. Walker points out that it doesn't matter if you don't sleep at all one night, or have just five hours sleep each night for five consecutive nights, the results are the same: our emotions swing about like they're on a pendulum. I can definitely relate to this when trying to pack up a tent after a rubbish night's sleep on a campsite!

TEENAGERS ARE PROGRAMMED TO SLEEP LATER

We know that the natural sleep patterns (the circadian rhythms) of children, adolescents and adults are different. Basically, teenagers are wired to go to sleep later and wake up later than adults – and 8:30 a.m. school start times are not exactly helpful for the adolescent brain.

Why the difference? Well, one hypothesis (Walker, 2018) is that when humans lived in tribes thousands of years ago, these different sleep patterns gave each tribe a better chance of surviving. Instead of the whole tribe slumbering and snoring for the same solid eight hours, having different sleep windows shortened the amount of time the tribe was vulnerable to attack. Another hypothesis is that by being programmed to feel sleepy later, teenagers got a couple of hours to go out into the night, on their own, to hunt, experience a bit of danger, and develop independence and confidence.

MELATONIN

Melatonin is a hormone that gets released at night and helps regulate the timing of when we sleep. It's commonly thought of as a sleeping aid – but it isn't. If we were about to board a sleep train, melatonin would be the conductor blowing a whistle to signal that it's time for the train to leave. The train's engine is other parts of the brain that generate sleep. Some people take melatonin pills, but as Walker (2018) points out, these are more likely to be helpful for their placebo effect – they are not 'sleeping pills'. In the morning, as the sun starts to rise, melatonin release is shut down. When we wake up, getting out of bed soon after and opening the curtains will help switch off the melatonin supply and help us stay awake.

LIGHT AND DEVICES

Because the onset of darkness helps to release melatonin, when we use electronic devices like tablets and phones the process is delayed and disrupted. In fact, researchers have found that reading an iPad reduces melatonin production by 50 per cent compared with reading a paper book, and it also delays the rise of melatonin by up to three hours (Walker, 2018). This makes it much harder for us to fall asleep. There is no doubt in researchers' minds that using blue light devices messes with our sleep. Stating these facts might encourage parents and carers to take a more active role in helping primary school-aged children get used to having devices out of their bedrooms at night. By the time they're teens, the habits have hardened...it's a bit late!

WHAT CHANGES HELP

There's strong evidence that cognitive behavioural therapy for insomnia (CBT-I) is much more effective than sleeping pills (Smith *et al.*, 2002), and lots of the lessons learnt in effective CBT-I are taught in low intensity CBT trainings. As practitioners, we're not just passing on 'sleep tips' – we're offering evidence-based advice. Here are some of the key sleep hygiene pointers, as recommended by Walker (2018) and Veale (2021).

- Stick to a sleep schedule. If you're falling asleep too late, then get up earlier, or move your alarm clock time gradually forward. We are creatures of habit, and it takes time to make changes. Spending less time in bed builds up 'sleep pressure' and means we will likely get to sleep more quickly the following night.

- Make sure your room is dark, your bed's comfortable, and you're not too warm.

- Exercise for at least 30 minutes a day, but don't do it late in the evening.

- Avoid caffeine and nicotine, particularly after mid-afternoon. Caffeine has a 'half-life' of five hours (Brachtel and Richter, 1992) so if you crack open a can of energy drink at 6 pm there'll still effectively be half a can's worth of caffeine keeping you alert at 11 pm.

- Get your melatonin switched off by opening the curtains as soon as you wake up. Get out of bed and do something active.

- As tempting as it might be, don't nap during the day.

- Avoid blue lights two hours before bedtime. Turn your phone to blue-light mode. Relax, and have time to wind down (no homework late at night!). This will help switch on melatonin production. Leave your phone out of your bedroom or put it on airplane mode.

- No clock watching at night. Turn your clock away from you. Keeping an eye on the time can increase the stress you feel about not being asleep.

- Trying to sleep – and feeling anxious about not falling asleep – can paradoxically make it harder to fall asleep. If you're lying in bed awake for more than 20 minutes, then get up, read a book, listen to a podcast or do something else relaxing until you start to feel sleepy.

HOW TO WORK WITH SLEEP HYGIENE

At the time of writing, researchers (Orchard *et al.*, 2019) are still developing a complete low intensity intervention for children and adolescents suffering poor sleep, but meanwhile we can follow some key steps that echo more established adult CBT-I interventions.

The key steps are:

1. Provide psychoeducation and check symptoms.

2. Check for motivation to make changes.

3. Help your client start a sleep diary.

4. Support your client to change their routines and behaviours.

5. Review – and if necessary use other interventions like worry-control techniques.

Before beginning any work, it's obviously helpful to work out how much poor sleep is affecting your client and establish a baseline to work from. We need a rough idea of when they fell asleep and woke up over the previous week to ascertain how many hours a night they're getting. Using a sleep diary and a checklist of symptoms (there are plenty available online) will help with this.

Working from what the client's told us, we can come up with a simple 'vicious circle' formulation of their sleep difficulties (Figure 16.1). Psychoeducation is then incredibly helpful. For example, explaining how teens are wired to go to bed later to help the survival of the tribe can help normalise some of the difficulty. We can then run through the top tips to sleep better, asking which might be easier or harder to implement.

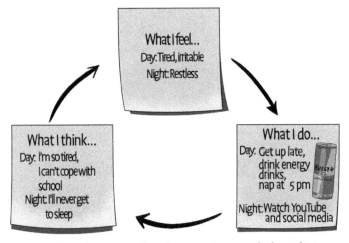

Figure 16.1: A common sleep hygiene vicious cycle formulation

Using a motivational interviewing grid (see Chapter 23) can be useful to understand the pros and cons of staying up late, and to determine what impact poor sleep is having on a young person. There may well be positives – staying up gaming or chatting with friends. It's also important to check your client's amount of motivation to improve their sleep before committing to a big change like leaving their phone out of their room. One way of framing it is to say, 'Is it worth just trying this as an experiment for two weeks and seeing if it does make you feel better during the daytime?'

Asking parents or young people to keep a weekly sleep diary will then help us keep track of how things go. Work together to problem solve and review what changes are being made.

Of course, some clients may be worrying excessively at night, and will need additional help managing their worries and stress levels – we touch briefly on this in Chapter 18. Having enough time to wind down and help our brains switch off can help with reducing worries on its own. Involving someone from the back-up team to help remind the young person to make these changes will make them more likely to stick. For example, if a young person is stressing about exams and cramming in hours and hours of revision late into the night, they may need a parent or carer to remind them that working late is often counter-productive.

If a young person says they're suffering frequent recurring nightmares then it's worth asking about if they've gone through any traumatic experiences – see Chapter 21 for some questions you could ask. Not everyone who has nightmares has PTSD, but it's worth checking out in case the young person needs more specialist support.

TAKE-AWAYS

▶ Sleep and emotional wellbeing have a circular relationship – one affects the other.

▶ The brain doesn't do as good a job at regulating emotions after a poor night's sleep.

▶ Teenagers naturally go to bed later and get up later than adults.

▶ Screens can really delay and disrupt sleep.

▶ Simple changes in habits – like getting up and going to bed at the same time every day – can be really helpful.

CHAPTER 17

Key Principles in Brief Behavioural Activation for Depression

The cruelty of what our minds can do 'for no reason' when we're depressed is so wonderfully captured by Arlo Parks in her song 'Black Dog'. So often it can feel that way, when we're locked in that horrible, depressed place, seemingly trapped, unable to find a way out to feel better. And there are no magic fixes. But helping a client see what's keeping their depression going can be the first of many important steps towards recovery. This chapter highlights the principles in brief behavioural activation (BA), a key intervention developed by Laura Pass and Shirley Reynolds, and gives some tips on how to make it most effective.

THIS CHAPTER COVERS:

- Why depression often slips under the radar in schools
- Different ways depression can affect young people
- Why and how BA works
- Why identifying and thinking about values is so important
- Recapping the key steps in BA
- A few words on rumination and cognitive approaches

UNDERSTANDING ADOLESCENT DEPRESSION

Depression is often missed in the school environment. One reason is that in a hectic classroom with 30 students, a teacher could be forgiven for not noticing if one pupil is a little quieter or more withdrawn. It's easy to just assume it's part of their character. A second reason is that depression in children and young people can look very different from low mood in adults – and also differs from one individual to another. In fact, two young people can have totally different presentations yet both be suffering from depression.

In terms of a diagnosis of depression, the key factors are low mood, irritability or a loss of interest in things (known in the psychiatric world as anhedonia). Other symptoms include sleep problems, appetite problems, cognitive problems, fatigue, suicidal thoughts, a feeling of worthlessness, and psychomotor retardation or agitation.

If a young person's ability to function has been impaired and they have experienced five of the above every day, for most of the day, over a period of at least two weeks then they qualify for a diagnosis. Of course, very few children actually get to see a psychiatrist who is able to give such a diagnosis, but it is worth bearing all this in mind because it teaches us just how many different ways depression can be present.

Let's think about two different young people. In the last two weeks 13-year-old Ava has looked more glum than usual. She's often by herself and hasn't wanted to see her friends at lunchtime at school. Ava's been complaining of feeling tired in the mornings, and her friends have said she's messaged them saying she's feeling worthless and can't see the point in going on.

Meanwhile Ava's classmate Noah, a keen striker with hopes of joining Liverpool, unexpectedly dropped out of football at the start of term. He's distracted and struggling to concentrate in class, and he's got into trouble recently with three different teachers after having outbursts in class. In fact, his Dad rang the school yesterday to say he'd seemed really agitated and fidgety, and hardly eaten – he's thinking of taking him to the GP.

Ava might fit our preconceptions of what depression commonly looks like – but Noah might well be depressed too. Does he remind you of anyone? Maybe that 15-year-old lad who stormed past you in the corridor yesterday? It's important we bear in mind the variety of ways depression can present to ensure we don't miss anyone who might need help.

The terms 'low mood' and 'depression' are sometimes used interchangeably. 'Low mood' sounds a bit less clinical, but 'depression' isn't just about feeling low – for teenagers it could be more about their loss of interest in things or irritability.

Table 17.1: The most common depressive symptoms

Symptoms	% of depressed young people with them
Sleep problems	91.8
Low mood	83.9
Concentration	75.1
Fatigue	73.3
Worthlessness	67.5
Anhedonia	65.2
Irritability	62.8
Suicidal ideation	60.9
Appetite	47.3
Psychomotor agitation	31.4

Source: Goodyer *et al.*, 2017

You can see from Table 17.1 (Goodyer *et al.*, 2017) that sleep problems are really common for teenagers with depression: nine out of ten have sleep disturbance. Recent thinking by experts including psychiatrist David Veale (2021) is that working on sleep hygiene at the same time or even before help with depression is recommended. Indeed, insomnia and depression have a circular relationship, impacting on each other – more on this in Chapter 16.

ADOLESCENT BRAIN DEVELOPMENT

As mentioned in Chapter 1, during adolescence the pre-frontal cortex is still growing at a rapid pace and the teen brain's 'executive functioning' development is incomplete. It's much harder for younger teens than adults to engage in 'meta-cognition' – thinking about thinking. When teenagers act in challenging ways or do something a bit daft, it's so common for frustrated parents to want to shout 'just think about it!' – but actually this isn't something that's easy for them to do!

Depression puts the boot in even harder by hammering a teenager's ability to concentrate, remember and focus. Research shows that this happens to three in every four depressed teenagers as shown in Table 17.1. Being less able to plan, organise or remember makes life even harder in a pressured academic environment. In terms of an MHST's whole school wellbeing approach, teachers working with depressed children and young people could helpfully be reminded that they may well have a reduced working memory and may benefit from adapted instructions, and so on.

SUICIDALITY

When assessing a depressed young person, we should keep an ear out for any beliefs about feeling like being a burden or finding it hard to reach out for help. As suicidality researcher Rory O'Connor (2019) says – when we're depressed, we can be so restricted in our thinking that it is almost impossible for us to think of alternatives. The road narrows.

So, if someone says 'I don't want to be a burden on others', treat this as an explicit invitation to ask about suicidal thoughts. In my experience, it's also very useful to normalise a difficulty in asking for help. We could frame it that people who don't want to trouble others are generally sensitive and kind souls. We could add that thinking you can't reach out will likely make you feel even more isolated and will make your depression even worse.

Because suicidal ideation is so common in depression (Cash and Bridge, 2009), Pass and Reynolds (2020) say it's essential we check in each and every session with how the young person is doing in this regard, asking about suicidal thoughts as part of our routine outcome measure questions. We also need to ask about any changes in planning or intent so we can keep the young person safe, and document this in our notes. Research has shown that asking explicit questions about risk does not increase risk (de Cou and Schumann, 2017). Hopefully this finding will make you feel a bit more confident in asking regularly.

WHY BEHAVIOURAL ACTIVATION?

NICE guidance (2019) advises offering either non-directive supportive therapy, group CBT, or guided self-help for low mood – with an additional recommendation to provide it within schools and the community. The evidence base for adult BA is growing (Pass, Brisco and Reynolds, 2015) and there are some promising early results for adolescent depression (McCauley *et al.*, 2015). So, within a school environment, a student with depression could helpfully be offered either counselling or guided self-help using CBT principles.

When it comes to the type of guided self-help we offer, it's important to be mindful of the difficulties a young person faces with their brain's reduced capacity for executive functioning and meta-cognition. Instead of a purely cognitive approach – for example, getting our client to review their negative thoughts and come up with more balanced ones – in BA we instead ask our client to experiment with doing different things in their week, with the aim being that it'll lead to them thinking and feeling differently. It's an 'outside-in' therapy, that acknowledges that what we do in our lives outside our heads will affect how we then feel in our heads. This is the opposite of 'inside-out', where we try to change our minds and feelings first, which then affects what we do in our lives.

It might sound a bit simplistic. But depression so often leads us to retreat under the bedcovers. We feel tired, we can't cope and so we do less. Generally, we then feel even worse. And this is part of how we stay depressed. It's not that we intend to feel worse, but we do. In fact, there are many 'unintended consequences' of things we commonly do when we're depressed – see Figure 17.1 for more of these.

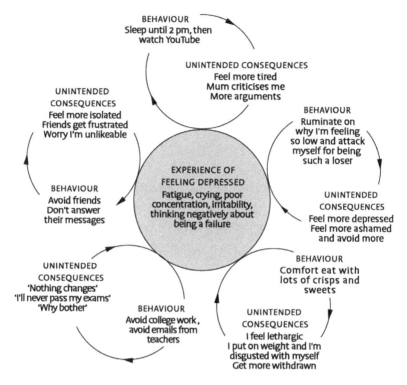

*Figure 17.1: A formulation of the unintended consequences of some
of the possible behaviours of a depressed Year 12 student*
Source: Based on Veale, 2008

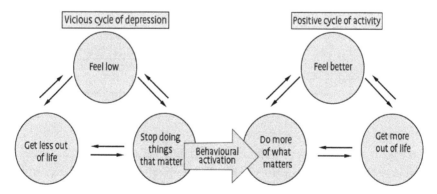

Figure 17.2: The brief behavioural model
Source: Pass and Reynolds, 2020

One way to attempt to lift our mood is by changing what we do (Figure 17.2). This helps us break that vicious cycle of inactivity. However hard it seems, having a plan to get more active can help shift our mood over time. As I write this, I have a mantra from Sussex University CBT lecturer Peter Garwood ringing in my ears: 'Stick to the plan, not to the mood!' Go out and do the stuff you planned to do, no matter how you feel. Don't follow what your mood and depressed thinking would have you do, but follow the plan you came up with that you think will help.

TRY IT OUT: explaining behavioural activation

Role play explaining the behavioural model of depression with a colleague, asking them for any examples of times they've felt low or depressed, and drawing out the BA vicious and positive cycles of activity.

THE IMPORTANCE OF VALUES IN BEHAVIOURAL ACTIVATION

As Laura Pass and Shirley Reynolds (2020) put it, it's not just about doing more, but doing *more of what matters*. If activities are really of value to a teenager, they're much more likely to give them a go and stick at them.

When you remember your time as a teenager, how many people asked you what really mattered to you? Actually, scratch that – when was the last time anyone ever asked you that at all?! In the hustle and bustle of GCSEs, A levels and all the rest, few teenagers are asked by an adult about what matters to *them*. Exploring values is a lovely way of getting to know someone.

It's pretty clear what matters to Greta Thunberg: saving the planet from the perils of climate change. Yet for several years as a young teenager, Greta was seriously depressed (BBC, 2019). She'd stopped going to school, stopped talking to her family, and began to refuse to eat. Her parents supported Greta's environmental campaigning principally because they could see just how much this mattered to Greta and thought it might help her recovery. Greta radically changed her life from schoolgirl to campaigner, sailing to UN climate summits and speaking out at events. Of course, not all young people are lucky enough to have such a supportive family, but nevertheless Greta's story is a great example of values-based BA in action.

Whether it's the environment, caring for others, concern for animals, social justice, a passion for a sport, religion, a desire to succeed in a particular career, a wish to travel or the joy of being with particular people, values come in many shapes and sizes.

And a teen's values may well feel very personal to them – or all too easily dismissed by the adults in their lives, resulting in them feeling misunderstood. For example, it's easy to be critical of someone wanting to spend an evening on an Xbox. But for them, it might be an important hour of social connection. Spending time with others is a value that young person is living out through gaming. It's helpful to use lists of values as featured in some BA manuals and books, or values cards. Pass and Reynolds (2020) recommend using the categories grid in Table 17.2 to help this exploration of values.

Table 17.2: What matters to me: my values grid

Me	Things that matter	People who matter
Hobbies/fun e.g. Xbox, shopping	Education e.g. doing well in English	Family e.g. my cousins
Physical health e.g. swimming, dance	Everyday stuff e.g. watching shows with sister	Friends e.g. Jameel and Kunal
Looking after myself e.g. getting enough sleep	The bigger picture e.g. Black Lives Matter	Important others e.g. dance teacher

THE STEPS IN BEHAVIOURAL ACTIVATION

BA can be broken down into six key steps.

Understanding the problem and normalising

We first need to understand how low mood is affecting our client's life. Asking your client to draw out a timeline looking at the ups and downs of their life to date is a good in-road for this task. Hopefully a timeline will help identify life events that triggered low mood. Looking at these onset and contributory factors can really help a young person understand why they might be depressed. Quite often young people think they're depressed because there's something wrong with them. Discussing the triggers can help shift this thinking towards a more helpful understanding that they're naturally depressed because of the tough things they've been through. It's a case of *'it's not about what's wrong with you, but what's happened to you'*. We can further help with this by telling them it's no wonder they feel like they do. You might wonder with them, *'Who wouldn't feel like you do given what you've been through?'*

Psychoeducation, and more normalising

Hopefully you'll now appreciate how important psychoeducation is when working with depression. Young people find it really helpful when we can normalise some of the common difficulties and experiences depressed people go through. One way of doing this is through looking at a list of depression symptoms together, ticking off the ones that apply to the young person and asking more about what it's like for them – and then helping them understand how things like tiredness, irritability and having no motivation are a direct result of depression. Another way of doing this is by spending lots of time going through a young person's answers to standardised questionnaires such as RCADs.

Pass and Reynolds (2020) encourage practitioners to involve the parent or carer in the first session or by phone so they get a better sense of what their young person is going through and can be more helpful later. If a parent understands the brief BA model and the maintenance factors, they'll be much better positioned to be able to help their young person as they try to change their weekly routine.

It's also helpful to normalise the fact that depression can make it hard to learn, remember and take things in (as mentioned in Chapter 9). That can affect how the therapy goes. In my experience with clinically depressed older teenagers I have had to slow the pace right down and check in after almost every exchange to ensure I'm being useful. By naming depression's effects and wondering about them with your client in the room, you're also helping to strengthen the working alliance.

We also need to spend sufficient time reiterating how normal and human it is to want to withdraw and do less when we're feeling low. Asking a client about a time they felt down and then did less and felt worse, and then drawing out that example to illustrate the vicious cycle of depression (see Figure 17.2), is an important part of this work. To help this normalisation, you could also perhaps talk about a celebrity who's been depressed and what kept the depression going.

Making the link between what we do and how we feel

It can be quite challenging for a young person to get to understand that there's often a link between what we do and how we feel. When you think about it, we never get taught this stuff and it can be quite hard to get your head round.

To help clients with this important learning point, Craig *et al.* (2012) incorporate a useful exercise in their BA manual. It involves the questions used in the following example.

Practitioner: Okay, I know you've been feeling depressed recently. Can you think about any times over the last week when you felt a bit worse in mood? Can you remember what you were doing?

Client: Yeah, I wasn't doing anything. I was sat in my bedroom worrying about all the work I had to do.

Practitioner: That sounds really hard. What do you think made you feel a bit worse?

Client: I just couldn't manage to get anything done so I felt really useless.

Practitioner: And thinking about that time, how much of a sense of achievement did you get when you were doing this, from 0 to 10, with 0 being no sense of achievement at all, and 10 being a huge sense of achievement?

Client: I'd say a three.

Practitioner: And from 0 to 10, how much of a sense of pleasure did you get when you were doing this?

Client: Probably a two.

Practitioner: Okay, thank you. And can you think about any times over the last week when you felt a bit better in mood. Can you remember what were you doing?

Client: Went to the shops with Mum and bumped into a friend. Had a chat together.

Practitioner: What made you feel a bit better?

Client: It was good to get out of the house. It was a nice surprise seeing the friend and I enjoyed talking to her.

Practitioner: And from 0 to 10, how much of a sense of achievement did you get when you were doing this?

Client: I guess around a four.

Practitioner: And how much of a sense of pleasure did you get when you were doing this?

Client: About a seven.

The point we're trying to help our clients understand is that *we're always doing something*. Even when I'm lying in bed, worrying about a group chat message – that's still doing something, and it will lead me to feel a certain way. And doing some things makes us feel better than others. Asking the above questions helps our client understand this crucial fact.

Diary keeping and activity logging

Keeping a diary of some sort helps our client record what they get up to and rate how they feel while doing it. It can be quite a chore, so one tip is to say that keeping a diary is a way of you getting to know them a bit better, because what we get up to says a little about who we are. Another tip is to say it's an experiment – to test out if what we do does affect how we feel.

Writing a paper diary is one approach – some young people prefer to take photos on their phones and record voice notes with them. Setting up reminders on phones can help.

There are different ways of recording how activities affect how we feel. Some activity logs encourage recording levels of achievement, closeness and enjoyment (ACE). Personally I prefer just 'pleasure' and 'achievement' as it's two things to record, rather than three. Pleasure is an obvious one – achievement less so. Clients often express surprise about how much a sense of achievement can contribute to their well-being. Things like tidying our room, finishing a piece of homework, cooking or folding our clothes are often under-appreciated compared with the instant dopamine hits of social media and gaming.

Finding out what matters

Next, it's important to spend time working out what matters to young people. It's about digging into the detail of what's really important, and then thinking creatively of weaving more of these 'core' values into day-to-day life. Again, core manuals and workbooks will include lists of different values. Once we've identified the values, we can then convert these into 'valued activities'.

So, for example, a client might really value their relationship with their granddad. The valued activity could be as simple as the client visiting their granddad once a week instead of once a month, or speaking to them on the phone for five minutes a day. For a perfectionist who has locked themselves into an overly gruelling revision routine, it could be spending 30 minutes on the Xbox in between study sessions. The value here is feeling relaxed and switching off from work, and the activity helps with this.

One 16-year-old a colleague worked with had a real passion for food and committed to cooking for his Mum and brother every day. Win-win all round! He really valued the creativity involved in cooking and also gained pleasure from seeing his Mum's pleasure.

After working out the things we do that we value, it's important that we break the activities into small steps that are achievable and engage with the young person to work out how to put them into action. As Reynolds (Pass and Reynolds, 2020) states, the activities will fail if they're too challenging, or they haven't got the support in place to make them happen. For example – if someone wants to join a dance club, but they haven't got the money for the bus to get across town – we're going to set them up to fail unless we can help problem solve a solution with them.

Activity scheduling and checking if the experiment is working

If you've managed to work with a young person who's been able to change up what they do in their week, congratulations! Keep encouraging them to log and rate their activities and see if the experiment works. Does spending more time on what matters to them improve their mood and wellbeing, or not? It's a case of problem solving, week by week, as quite often making small changes is not as easy in practice as it might appear in session. It's often helpful to refer back to the young person's back-up team as you go with this. If it isn't working for any reason, then you will need to do some problem solving – see Chapter 23 for more on this. After these steps, we would move into blueprinting work (see Chapter 22) to help our client ensure the changes are maintained.

BEHAVIOURAL ACTIVATION SUMMARY

BA, as Shirley Reynolds says, *is simple but not easy* (Pass and Reynolds, 2020). There's a lot to it that could be easily missed if you dozed off in the lectures or just skim-read the manuals. Try it out for yourself and see if it works. Then try it on a friend. And then go for it with young people. Given the underlying principles of BA, it's unlikely not to work a little, if the young person is able to engage with the sessions and has enough hope and motivation to make changes. Of course, if it isn't working or the young person is deteriorating then be really mindful of continuing to monitor risk, discuss the case in supervision and consider referring to a more specialist service (see Chapters 14 and 23).

COGNITIVE CHALLENGES IN DEPRESSION

Rumination

As Davide Veale (2008) says, if you ask someone to spend ten minutes thinking and talking about their depression, chances are they'll end up feeling more depressed. Rumination and a spiral of self-attacking self-talk are common facets of depression, where the mind turns in on itself. Among other things, it involves us asking questions that can't be answered, beating ourselves up and wondering 'why me?' The brain is spinning like a hamster on a wheel, going over and over the same difficult thoughts. By keeping its focus on the difficulty, our minds think they're trying to help but actually the process makes things worse.

It's helpful to use an analogy when describing rumination. You could say the mind can be a bit like a car's wheel stuck in the mud (Figure 17.3), spinning like crazy and flicking muck up everywhere but not actually helping the car move. Or you could describe it as a washing machine, stuck on spin cycle. 'The goal is to acknowledge the thoughts but not to attempt to stop or control or answer back at them,' explains Veale (2008, p.33). We need to recognise when we've got our foot on the pedal and we're making the problem worse and then do something differently – putting out attention on something outside our minds.

Figure 17.3: The spinning wheel analogy is useful when talking about rumination

Thinking traps

Alongside BA, some basic psychoeducation on common 'thinking traps' can be very helpful for many young people, too. In CAMHS groups, we've found it effective to run through these with young people and parents or carers together. I've never once met anyone who hasn't fallen prey to several of the 'thinking traps', and it can be normalising for children to hear parents talk about their own.

The important thing is to realise we all catastrophise, we all mind-read, we all think in all-or-nothing terms, we all totally blame ourselves for things, and we all do these things to a much greater degree when we're down on ourselves and feeling hopeless and low. When children hear that their parents suffer in this way too it can be hugely helpful and make them feel much more a part of the human race.

If I only had time to introduce just one cognitive change technique it would be this: to learn to ask yourself, *'Is this me talking, or my depression?'* It's a way of quickly externalising the 'black dog' of depression. The black dog is the problem – not you. This simple step can sometime help reduce a lot of the negative thinking style's power. The other important point to reinforce is the need to follow the plan, rather than the mood. This can help someone see beyond the self-limiting thoughts generated by the depressed thinking style.

TAKE-AWAYS

► Depression can 'look' very different between different young people, and irritability and anhedonia (loss of interest in things) are often-missed symptoms of depression in adolescents.

► When assessing, always be mindful of risk, in particular thoughts around being a burden.

► From what we know about how depression affects the adolescent brain, a behavioural approach makes a lot of sense, and the emerging evidence for BA is promising.

► Time spent helping a young person understand the link between what we do and how we feel is time well spent.

► It's important to understand a young person's values if we're to help them flourish. It's not just about doing more – it's about doing more of what matters.

► The 'spinning wheel' is a useful analogy for rumination. It's useful to normalise negative thoughts, and help a young person think about how they can notice them, but not get sucked into a vortex of rumination and self-attack so common in depression. What could they do differently?

CHAPTER 18

Key Principles in Graded Exposure for Anxiety

Supporting young people to gradually face their fears and develop confidence is a powerful way to help them overcome anxiety. Clinical experience shows us that its success is underpinned by really good psychoeducation. If our clients can grasp what anxiety is and understand the rationale behind facing up to fears they're far more likely to be willing and engaged with the work.

THIS CHAPTER COVERS:

- How to help clients better understand their anxieties
- How avoidance and reassurance can make anxiety worse
- Why graded exposure works
- Analogies to help clients understand safety behaviours and coping tools
- The basics of different approaches for specific kinds of anxiety

---

UNDERSTANDING ANXIETY

Figure 18.1: Illustrator Cara Bean asked her friends, 'what does anxiety feel like in the body?' and drew out their answers. Copyright 2021, Cara Bean.[1]

Never underestimate how crippling anxiety can be: it's often a truly horrible, debilitating experience, and Cara Bean's cartoons (Figure 18.1)

---

1 These images were excerpted from http://patreon.com/CaraBeanComics. Previous comics by the author include Let's Talk About It: A Graphic Guide to Mental Health and Snake Pit: Notes on Adolescent Suicide and Depression. Both resources are available for free online.

capture some ways anxiety can feel. Anxiety can make us feel very alone, or like we're going mad, but understanding that the physical responses are our bodies' natural way of getting ready for danger can be so reassuring. Anxiety is something we can all experience, and it's hard wired into our machinery as a survival instinct. Our very natural response is to avoid anxiety-making situations and run for the hills – and that's why it is so important our clients understand why doing the opposite is fundamental to recovery. It's a huge deal to be asked to try to work through it – and never forget that!

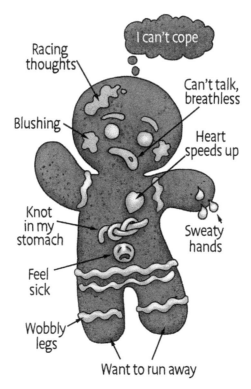

Figure 18.2: The gingerbread man exercise – so useful for anxiety psychoeducation

One way of normalising anxiety is by talking about common anxiety-making experiences and how they affect us – there are plenty of videos online of performers getting stage fright, or animals in documentaries responding to dangerous situations. We could also do a little careful self-disclosure. A colleague often starts his anxiety workshops by drawing attention to sweat patches showing through his shirt, and then explains some of his physical experiences of performance anxiety. Obviously, we don't want to make the session about ourselves, but talking about some experiences of anxiety can be really helpful.

Drawing and writing symptoms out on a simple gingerbread man shape (Figure 18.2) can help a young person link their own feelings with what we know about anxiety. A good way to start separating out thoughts from feelings is to draw thought bubbles coming out from the head. It's like separating out your socks and pants in your laundry: stick the thoughts into the bubbles and put the feelings and body sensations into the different parts of the body where they're felt. Prompt questions could include:

'When you were in the bus feeling stressed, how did you feel in your body?'

'What was it like in your tummy – did you notice any funny feelings?'

'Were your hands and feet all relaxed or stressed and bunched up?'

'Could you think clearly or was your mind all jumbled up or racing about?'

'What went through your mind?'

Explaining the flight, fight and freeze or 'flop' response is important, too. The amygdala is the part of the brain that's most responsible for our survival over the last few thousands of years. It makes us jump out of the way of passing buses and take our hands off hot surfaces without us even having to think. It can make us freeze and go very still – like a rabbit in headlights – or flop and retreat from others. Of course, it also can help us get geared up for a confrontation. We don't have much choice in how it chooses to respond, but we certainly notice it in our bodies. If we're ready to take flight, we'll notice our heart racing as it pumps more blood out to the muscles ready for them to work, and it'll make us want to pee and evacuate our bowels to lighten us up before we have to run.

And when we think about adolescents and children, Vicki Curry reminds us it's also important to remember that their stage of brain development means they tend to operate more in the 'here and now' and think less about consequences than adults. It can be harder for them to 'ride out' anxiety.

It might also help to remind clients that the human race has survived because of anxiety, not in spite of it! If we never felt anxious, we'd get run over or fall off a cliff pretty early on in our lives. Anxiety does a great job of keeping us safe. It can be nice to point this out in an anxiety workshop or group – instead of being a group of anxiety sufferers, we could reframe it that we're a room full of born survivors wired to succeed and, in terms of evolution, the anxious gene will always win through.

However, be mindful that not everyone will be comfortable with us talking about evolution. Vicki Curry suggests we say 'we are designed' rather than 'we are designed by evolution'. When clients hold religious views such as creationism, there are still ways of talking about anxiety and the brain in helpful ways. Kolts (2016) suggests we say the brain still has some glitchy bits, and that while our brains worked in ways that helped our ancestors living in the forests with danger lurking round every corner, they don't always work so well in the modern world. It's possible to work together even holding very different beliefs – you could explain the glitches by wondering if, for your client, *our tricky brains are a riddle that God has given us to figure out* (Kolts, 2016, p.9).

When talking about how the amygdala works, smoke alarms are a useful metaphor. Some houses have very sensitive smoke alarms, and you can't turn the grill on without the alarm immediately wailing. Others have old ones that'll only go off when you can't see the room for smoke. If the house was a brain, then our amygdala is the equivalent of the smoke alarm. We're all wired differently, and some have more sensitive smoke alarms than others, meaning our amygdala will activate more quickly and be more responsive to signals of danger.

Last, we need our clients to understand that our brains can't tell between real and imagined threats. The human brain is an incredible thing. But when it comes to anxiety it is actually a bit basic and prone to malfunctioning. All animals build associations about threats that help them survive. A lizard might shed its tail when threatened. A cat will puff up into a big ball to make itself look scarier. And after time, we build the same kind of associations in our minds. Research suggests we have highly developed abilities to envisage future threats (Mobbs *et al.*, 2015). However, the part of the brain that activates us and gets us ready for action reacts in a similar way whether the threat is real or imagined (Suddendorf and Corballis, 2007). That's why we get this huge, sometimes overwhelming, physiological response to danger, regardless of whether it's a cyclist hurtling towards us on the pavement, or the sight of the school gates, or a clown, or a plate of food. If an association with danger has been built, the response is strong!

It's likely that you'll find yourself working with young people who've suffered anxiety attacks in class. Sometimes a young person will hear a loud noise in class – a chair falling over or similar – and feel panic. Afterwards, after realising it was something innocuous, the young person might still find herself feeling edgy and scanning the room for signs of danger. She might find it really helpful to hear about how these hard-wired instincts were designed to keep our ancestors alert to threats from wild animals in the forests they lived in. Scanning between the trees for movement kept them safe. But by continuing to be vigilant for signs of threat, we end up staying in that anxious state. Indeed, researchers now know that after envisaging a threat we rapidly increase alertness and environmental surveillance (Suddendorf and Corballis, 2007). We respond as if the threat is right around the corner.

Never underestimate how valuable psychoeducation like this is. As EMHP Suzanne Everill reflects, 'My best sessions are those when I can get a key point across such as fight, flight or freeze.' 'I can see that the client has suddenly really understood what's happening to them when they experience those awful physical symptoms, and you can sense their relief when they realise they're not alone and it's normal.'

UNDERSTANDING HOW AVOIDANCE MAKES ANXIETY WORSE

The next stage of the work is to help a client understand that responding to the threat by avoiding it makes us feel a bit better pretty quickly. We're out of danger – we can breathe! But the next time we approach that threat, it's likely our anxiety will be just as bad. Without meaning to, we are teaching our 'warning systems' that yes, indeed, we can't cope with that threat – it's a serious one and it needs avoiding.

Can you think of any examples in your life when you've done this? For myself, after I'd fallen out with a friendship group in my teens I remember I started feeling anxious about going to social things on my own, and I ended up making excuses and not going. After I'd done this a few times, I found it even harder to go to any social event. I'd taught myself that evenings out and barbecues were indeed things to be feared.

Some of the ways we avoid anxiety are quite subtle, like planning how to avoid the anxiety-provoking situation or focusing on the physical symptoms and trying to think out how to minimise them or avoid feeling them. However, these responses still maintain our focus on the threat itself. This response teaches us that avoidance is the means to survive the threat. This is called negative reinforcement – it's that fusion of the threat and response that makes our minds link them together and make them seem really real.

UNDERSTANDING WHY FACING OUR FEARS CAN HELP

Back in the dark ages, therapists used to just chuck their patients into whatever trigger situation made them feel super-anxious and let them scream it out. This is called 'flooding' and researchers learnt that it doesn't work so well. Instead, we do it in a gradual, step-by-step way, hence the 'graded' in 'graded exposure'. Very recently, there's been lots of re-thinking on why this works. Researchers now believe the most important aspect is that people learn they can cope with situations they once feared (Creswell, Waite and Hudson, 2020).

It's about learning that the fear can be withstood, and that if you stay in the feared situation gradually your amygdala comes back down off high alert. By doing so, we gently begin to calm our physiological response and begin to learn, 'Hey, maybe I *can* cope with this'. This is called 'inhibitory learning'. We work out we can survive, and as we do so, new associations are formed between the situation and us being okay. These new associations compete with the old associations between the situation and the sense of threat. As such, each step taken in facing the fear is an opportunity to learn and develop.

This approach is about deliberately going towards the anxiety, letting ourselves feel it and letting it come and go. It's a little like a process of uncoupling one half of a train from another. The back half of the train – the threat – gets decoupled from the front half – your mind's belief that it can't cope with that threat. Then the front half can move off down the track, leaving the fear behind.

Graded exposure breaks the cycle of escape and avoidance, which, buried deep in our core survival instincts, is keeping the cogs of anxiety turning. In the short term, escape produces some relief. We don't end up doing that thing we were anxious about. Long-term avoidance only makes our anxiety about the situation worse. It gives our minds proof that the threat is real.

The anxiety equation below (adapted from Mooney; see Padesky, 2020b) can help explain how facing our fears is helpful. It helps show how anxiety is directly related to both how much we overestimate the amount of danger and also how much we underestimate our ability to cope or the resources at our disposal.

$$\text{Anxiety} = \frac{\text{the perceived size of the threat or danger}}{\text{your confidence in your ability to cope}}$$

The steps involved in a graded exposure intervention are covered comprehensively in low intensity trainings, but to recap, they include:

- psychoeducation about anxiety and formulating the client's difficulty – as above

- identifying which problem to work on in particular and setting goals (see Chapter 6)

- identifying any safety behaviours – also known as 'unhelpful habits' (see below)

- working out any coping tools that will be helpful (see Chapter 20)

- drawing up a back-up plan (see Chapter 15)

- working out a plan of 'facing my fears' steps (also known as a fear hierarchy)

- working through the steps, week by week, problem solving any issues along the way and learning through doing

- at the end, blueprinting to ensure progress is maintained (see Chapter 22).

▩ TRY IT OUT: avoidance and facing our fears

Using your manual or worksheets, role play with a colleague how you might explore with a teenager how avoiding a situation can keep anxiety going, then explain how graded exposure can help.

BUILDING A 'FACING MY FEARS' HIERARCHY

As we face our fears, our bodies and minds get accustomed to surviving the threat. As Eelen and Vervliet (2006) put it, habituation is a process where a fear reaction triggered by a stimulus reduces in strength or even goes completely. This is when drawing out the habituation curve (Figure 18.3) is useful – most manuals and session-by-session plans include these. Our confidence that we can cope slowly builds, and the threat doesn't seem so big. Keep doing this and the anxiety should shrink, week by week. Of course, we also now know that it's not just about habituation – the 'inhibitory learning', or as I prefer to call it 'the-realising-you-can-survive-stuff-cognitive-aspect' is the most important bit (Creswell *et al.*, 2020). But the habituation curve can still capture both the physical and cognitive shifts that happen with graded exposure.

It's important to start on relatively easy tasks that help our client get a taste of anxiety, but not find the task so challenging it puts them off the intervention completely. Let's use the example of a client who is scared of dogs, after getting bitten by one.

The first step could be to look at a cartoon picture of a dog, together, for two minutes in the session. You could use the 'fear rocket' metaphor and encourage your client just to ride the feeling out. The home practice could be for the client to do this themselves each day for the rest of the week and note down what they've learnt each time.

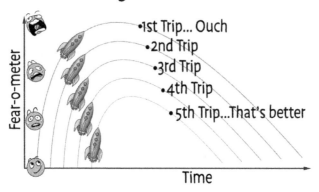

Figure 18.3: We can explain habituation by using a 'riding the fear rocket' metaphor. Each time we take a trip, the fear rocket climbs a little less high and the trip is shorter. We just need to stay with the rocket till it starts descending

A second step could be to watch a cartoon video of a dog on YouTube for five minutes a day.

Then you could work up to videos of real dogs, and then maybe involve meeting a neighbour who the client knows has a friendly, chilled dog.

If you can't think of five or six different steps to make a complete hierarchy ladder, you can increase and decrease intensity by making each planned activity either shorter or longer in time. And if a client finds a step too challenging, you can stay with it but reduce the time on it.

There are lots of creative ways of building a fear hierarchy. Most manuals and handouts use the 'ladder' as the template, but if your young person is into gaming, why not use a platforming video game template (see Figure 18.4)? The really important thing is to review each step and ask the client what they've learnt through the experiment – this will help reinforce their newly found sense of being able to cope, bit by bit. This cognitive restructuring has been proven to significantly accelerate treatment, according to Creswell *et al.* (2020).

My Missions

Boss Level Mission:..........................
Coping Skill:.........................
Unhelpful Habit to Drop:..........................
Bonus for Completing:..........................

Level 4 Mission: ....
Coping Skill:.........................
Unhelpful Habit to Drop:..........................
Bonus for Completing:..........................

Level 3 Mission: ....
Coping Skill:.........................
Unhelpful Habit to Drop:..........................
Bonus for Completing:..........................

Level 2 Mission: ....
Coping Skill:.........................
Unhelpful Habit to Drop:..........................
Bonus for Completing:..........................

Level 1 Mission: ....
Coping Skill:.........................
Unhelpful Habit to Drop:..........................
Bonus for Completing:..........................

Figure 18.4: Most young people don't climb ladders that often, but nearly all play video games. This is a creative way of drawing out a 'facing our fears' action plan

UNDERSTANDING SAFETY BEHAVIOURS

It's really important to understand if our client is engaging in any 'safety behaviours', but these can be a little confusing to understand. A safety behaviour is something we do to try to keep safe. For young people it might be things like:

- avoiding specific lessons or situations like having to speak in class

- scanning for danger – or the opposite, avoiding eye contact

- escaping from a situation at the first sign of feeling afraid

- distracting yourself from difficult thoughts or feelings, or trying to push them away

- asking others for reassurance.

They all make total sense and work in the short term, but in the long term they can keep the anxiety going. By carrying out safety behaviours we're treating anxiety as a serious problem that needs 'doing something about'. This reinforces a sense that you might not cope without doing it...and it might mean the anxiety might keep coming back more frequently. Of course though, everyone is different – it's about working out if it's helpful or hindering for the client. Let's think through safety behaviours by using a case example.

Nadiya's safety behaviours

Chef and TV celebrity Nadiya Hussain has suffered anxiety and panic attacks throughout her life. In the BBC show 'Nadiya: Anxiety and Me', clinical psychologist Paul Salkovskis helps Nadiya identify the things she does consciously and unconsciously to keep herself safe from danger.

Paul identifies how Nadiya drives everywhere for fear of meeting anyone, never does anything spontaneous and wouldn't dream of trying to go anywhere on public transport.

But Nadiya's got to a point in her life where she's a bit sick of feeling anxious. After a couple of sessions, Paul gently encourages her to try something out – a spontaneous trip to London!

Next thing, they're walking out of the clinic, down the road and into Oxford train station.

As Nadiya walks onto the busy platform she keeps her head down, avoiding eye contact. Paul encourages her to look up and look around her – to address her perceived threats, stay with the anxiety, let it subside and disconfirm the threat's value.

After ten minutes on the train Nadiya is beaming – she has done it – she's on a spontaneous day trip!

Later, we see Nadiya walk onto stage to give a live cooking demonstration to thousands of people.

'I'm very short-sighted,' she tells the audience, 'and normally I don't wear my glasses because I don't think I'll cope with seeing you all, but today I'm going to put them on! I feel sick with nerves but wow – look how lovely you all look!'

▨ TRY IT OUT: spotting safety behaviours
What were Nadiya's safety behaviours?

METAPHORS TO EXPLAIN WHY SAFETY BEHAVIOURS DON'T HELP

As safety behaviours are a little hard to understand, it can help to use metaphors and analogies. Here are two ideas.

Crocodiles

Imagine you've moved into a new street, and there's a neighbour who scatters salt outside his front door every morning (see Figure 18.5). One day, you ask him why he does this, and he replies, 'To stop the crocodiles'. When you say, 'But there are no crocodiles,' he replies, 'Of course there aren't, because I keep the salt topped up every day and it keeps them away.'

You can see why it makes sense for the man to keep doing this, but by doing it, he'll never learn that the crocodiles won't come. He's left at the mercy of what he thinks keeps him safe, and he'll keep doing it, and probably keep worrying that crocodiles are around the corner, too. (This metaphor is derived from one used by Waite and Williams, 2009.)

Figure 18.5: The crocodiles metaphor
Source: Adapted from Waite and Williams, 2009

Cats

Male cats quite often spray to mark their territory – it makes them feel safe. Let's say you've got a cat called Milo. Milo's always been pretty chilled, but in the last few weeks he's been getting stressed. A neighbour's cat keeps coming in your house and nicking Milo's food so Milo has started weeing in corners of the kitchen to mark his territory and ward the thief off. You get a bit sick of cleaning up the wee and to stop the thieving neighbour you decide to put a microchip cat-flap in, so only Milo can get in and out with his unique chip. Other cats are now barred from entry. However, it's likely Milo will keep spraying indoors even when the other cat can't get in. Milo believes it's only safe when your house stinks of his wee, and he'll keep feeling anxious when the smell dies down so will keep spraying! Milo's safety behaviour is keeping his cycle of anxiety going.

EXPLAINING COPING TOOLS AND STRATEGIES

Coping tools are different from safety behaviours. They are aids to help us face our fears, but we'll drop them over time. For example, if we're learning to swim we might use arm bands or a float. We'll definitely start at the shallow end of the pool and work our way up. Eventually we'll be on our own in deep water – the floats and shallow water were just tools to help us cope as we learnt. Another good example that many young people can relate to is learning to ride a bike. When we start, we might use stabilisers or a balance bike without pedals, and once we've got the hang of that, we'll move onto a proper bike. Equally, if the young person knows anyone who's broken a leg, you could talk about how they had to use a crutch for a bit until they were strong enough to walk again.

It's okay to use some tools to help us get through the times we feel anxious (see Chapter 20 for some ideas) but we need to remember that they're just temporary tools, and we don't want to hang on to them too long otherwise we might feel we can't swim, bike or walk without them. It's also important to distinguish between coping tools and safety behaviours. While an explosion in mindfulness colouring books and fiddle toys in school pastoral offices is in some ways a lovely thing, they can become problematic when young people think they can only manage if they have them – they might become safety behaviours that keep the problem going.

PANIC, GENERALISED ANXIETY, SOCIAL ANXIETY AND ANXIOUS THOUGHTS

Graded exposure is a common treatment component for a wide variety of different kinds of anxiety. Wherever avoidance is unwittingly helping to keep the anxiety going, exposure is likely to be useful. However, there are lots of other tools and techniques we can teach young people who are struggling with other kinds of anxiety where supplementary interventions are useful – and no doubt they've been covered in your trainings. If you're newer to it all, then here's a brief run-down on other kinds of anxiety. Kings College London and The Anna Freud Centre generously provide free manuals that dovetail with their main adolescent anxiety manual for all the following.

Panic

Panic is a feeling of extreme anxiety – it's really intense and can feel extremely frightening. Often people misinterpret their shallow breathing and heart rate and think they're having a heart attack. In fact, this misinterpretation can increase the sense of panic. Cognitive behavioural interventions with panic include trying not to avoid situations, and then trying to ground yourself and remind yourself you're safe. Some schools of thought say that slowing your breathing down is helpful, whereas others disagree and say this can become a safety behaviour that can actually make panic attacks more frequent.

Generalised anxiety disorder

Some people tend to worry about worries, which at its most severe can become 'generalised anxiety disorder' (GAD). When helping with this problem, it's important to acknowledge that it is the mind's tendency to worry that is the issue. We're not working to help a young person overcome every single anxious thought that pops into their head. Instead, we use a tool like a 'worry tree' as an action plan to help them do things differently when they notice a worry. Another useful tool is the 'doughnut of control' (see Figure 18.6), where we write down all the things we can't do in the ring of the doughnut, and the things we can in the middle. This can help separate out what we can work on and what we have to try to let go of. In fact, if you're in the middle of writing an assignment and feeling overwhelmed, why not give one a go now? In some services, GAD is treated by high intensity CBT therapists rather than low intensity practitioners.

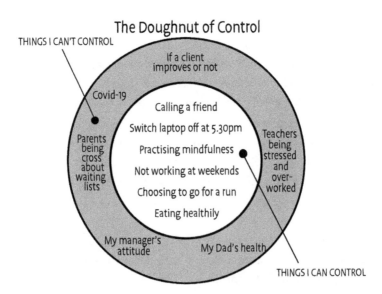

Figure 18.6: The doughnut of control exercise

Social phobia

Social phobia, or social anxiety disorder (the terms are interchangeable), might require additional treatment components where the client is encouraged to deliberately shift their awareness from how they're feeling out onto what's going on around them. The therapist might also encourage the client to take part in some video experiments, rating how they think they come across compared with how they actually come across, to disprove some of their unhelpful beliefs about themselves (e.g. 'I go 100 per cent red in the face and look totally embarrassing!'). Attention training is also useful to help clients learn to put their focus on external stimuli like music in order to turn down their dial on their internal self-evaluation chatter. Again, social phobia is sometimes treated by high intensity therapists as the treatment is a little more specialised.

Anxious thoughts

If anxious thoughts are really strong, then cognitive work may also be helpful. We can help young people to learn to spot anxious thoughts and to try to treat them differently either as clouds in the sky, letting them drift on by, or by reappraising them. The motto for this work is 'thoughts aren't necessarily facts'. In parent-led work, we help parents and carers assist their children to spot and investigate their anxious thoughts and give things a go anyway (Cresswell *et al.*, 2017). With teenagers, CBT therapists sometimes use thought records and other similar cognitive interventions to help those suffering really bad anxious thoughts, but for many young people just using helpful reminders and coping statements can be enough. The latter should be kept well stocked in our low intensity tool kits.

Summary

To summarise, facing fears is not the only tool for working with anxiety. But it is a good 'active ingredient' when working with the majority of anxious clients in early intervention work. As always, talk with your supervisor if you have doubts about your client's presentation, because getting the formulation right is crucial...and not always easy! Psychoeducation is so important with anxiety – and it's best done with frequent checking for understanding as you go, because while we might get very familiar with this stuff and trot it out like a shopping list, they are quite alien concepts for most people. But once a client 'gets it' we're often halfway there in terms of the work that needs doing to help them get better.

TAKE-AWAYS

► Generally, clients find it really helpful to understand the physiology of anxiety. It can help clients feel more human, and it also helps everyone understand why facing our fears is an important part of not letting anxiety win.

► Honour your client's experience of anxiety. It can be a horrible experience regardless of the trigger – whether it's buttons, balloons or sharks.

► The physiological response, and drive to avoid, is the same regardless of whether the threat is real or imagined.

► It's good to remember that anxiety develops when we overestimate threat and underestimate our ability to deal with it.

► If you stay with the fear it will eventually subside. If we set a meaningful goal, and work towards it, we habituate ourselves to the anxiety and also learn we can cope.

► Parents, carers and teachers can all collude in helping the young person avoid situations, unwittingly making the anxiety stick around longer than it otherwise might.

► Other tools are useful for particular kinds of anxiety, like generalised anxiety, social anxiety and panic. If the anxiety is mainly driven by anxious thoughts, then we can add in some cognitive work, too, but with young people try to keep it as simple as possible to start with.

CHAPTER 19

Key Principles in Parent-Led CBT for Anxiety

Supporting parents and carers rather than working with children directly is proving to be an efficient and effective way of helping younger children with anxiety. Cathy Creswell and Lucy Willetts have developed a fantastic six-session low intensity intervention, based on their book *Helping Your Child with Fears and Worries* (2019). This model is covered in full in their therapist manual (Halldorsson *et al.*, 2019), but this approach might be new to you. This chapter introduces the approach and then delves into some key tips on how to deliver it effectively.

THIS CHAPTER WILL COVER:

- The philosophy and principles of brief parent-led work
- The dynamics between children and parents that can influence a child's anxiety
- The importance of encouraging, normalising, validating and educating as we progress through the intervention

ABOUT THE APPROACH

'I had no idea that telling my son they'd be okay and not to worry was the wrong thing to do!' said a parent on her second session of parent-led CBT. 'I get it now – we don't want to diminish their feelings; we want them to learn they'll be alright in the end.'

Working directly with parents, rather than the children with the difficulty, might seem like an odd idea. After enjoying several years of work in primary schools I was definitely resistant to the idea – mainly because young children are such fun to work with! But when we have such a short amount of time to offer, skilling up parents so they can help their children overcome anxiety definitely makes sense.

Let's consider what the research (Murray, Cresswell and Cooper, 2009) tells us about the factors that contribute to a child's anxiety and how parent-led CBT fits with it. The factors they identify include:

- a child's genes and temperament

- life events that can affect a child

- how a child learns by the example of those around them

- how a child learns from how others respond and react to them

- how a child has been able to cope with different experiences in life.

The Cresswell approach focuses on the bottom three, homing in on the systemic factors. One of the key aims is to 'increase the parent's confidence in their ability to help their child overcome their difficulties with anxiety' (Halldorssen *et al.*, 2019, p.9). We also help parents identify any ways in which they're inadvertently helping keep their child's anxiety going – before moving on to 'modifying reinforcement cycles within the family' (Cresswell, 2021). The approach is underpinned by a recognition that parents usually know their children best and can adapt a practitioner's suggestions to make them work most effectively.

Parent-led CBT involves four main activities. The first is providing psychoeducation, including how anxiety develops in children and how we can help them overcome it. This includes talking about both the more helpful and less helpful ways a parent can respond. Second, we help parents learn how to help their children identify and examine anxious thoughts. We wonder with them if there might there be other ways of looking at things and look at the value of doing things differently, focusing on the importance of children 'having a go' in order to build their confidence. Third, we facilitate the family to think of goals linked to the child's anxieties and identify steps for them to work towards their goals.

Last, we teach problem-solving skills so parents can support their child to learn how to deal with life's difficulties and overcome obstacles.

THE JOB OF PARENTING

Parenting is often described as the toughest job in the world. Before we explore some key ways of making sessions successful, let's have a quick think first though of what life is like for parents, using a case example.

A case example

Last night Bozena dropped her nine-year-old daughter Lena off for her first evening at a new football club. Lena didn't know anyone else there and was feeling nervous as they got closer. As they pulled up in the car park, Lena said she felt sick and didn't want to get out of the car.

'Listen Lena, feeling nervous is totally normal when we try new things,' said Bozena. 'It'd be weird if you didn't feel some butterflies. I did ask you three times if you wanted to go this week and you said "yes" each time. I think you should go and find out if you enjoy it, and if you don't, well we don't have to go next week. Okay?'

Lena slinked off to join the others on the pitch. Bozena watched, feeling really sorry for Lena, and guilty for pushing her to go. She remembered all the times she'd felt anxious as a child herself. It took every ounce of effort to not run after her.

Welcome to the life of a parent: guilt, anxiety and feeling unsure about your decisions just as soon as you've made them! But as psychoanalyst Donald Winnicott (1963) first suggested, part of a parent's job is to learn to tolerate the feelings of their children and not lose themselves in their children's feelings – for at least most of the time. Parents need to be 'good enough', as he puts it. It's not easy tolerating anxiety in our children, particularly with so much awareness in the media around mental health and an increased understanding of how childhood experiences can shape us.

WHAT HELPS IN PRACTICE

Let's look at some common tips to help get parents on board and engaged with this work. It's no easy task, as often parents can feel attacked or criticised, even when they are genuinely wanting help and trying their best. The next section assumes you've been trained in this approach and are following the therapist's manual, supported by your supervisor.

GETTING THE PARENTS ON BOARD

As we all know, it's not easy asking for help. Our first job is to get alongside the parents. They may well be feeling deskilled or hopeless, vulnerable about feeling judged, sceptical or ambivalent. A good way to show you're on their side is to spend a proper amount of time encouraging parents to tell their story.

As Zoe Goode says, 'Quite often when meeting teachers, parents get a very short window and might not feel listened to. Be curious and let them ask lots of questions.'

We then need to acknowledge how hard it can be trying to parent an anxious child and set out our stall. One way to do this is to just state that all children are different and have unique challenges. 'I say that some kids are more complex to parent and support than others, and as wellbeing practitioners we can help them develop the advanced skills they might find helpful,' says Zoe.

It's then important to sell just how successful this intervention can be – particularly if parents would actually rather you just saw their child separately and didn't involve them! After identifying the parents' goals for their child, really link in how this approach can help with those particular goals, and drum in the importance of them fully committing to the sessions and doing the in-between session work too. It might help to explain the years of research that have gone into the programme and what the studies show.

Last, parents need to have grabbed a copy of *Helping Your Child with Fears and Worries* (Cresswell and Willetts, 2019). It's available at libraries and on the 'reading well' prescription list.[1] If there are barriers

---

1   https://reading-well.org.uk/books/books-on-prescription

to this, we need to be adaptive and get the information across in other ways. There are lots of fantastic psychoeducation videos freely available online, and we can also use techniques like drawing out a gingerbread man (Figure 18.2 in Chapter 18). Lots of practitioners recommend doing this psychoeducation with the parent and child together in the first session – it helps to embed a shared understanding of anxiety and normalises it as something we all experience.

UNDERSTANDING MAINTENANCE FACTORS

When a parent understands the maintenance factors that are keeping her child's anxiety going it's often a 'lightbulb' moment in the course of the intervention.

The therapist manual (Halldorsson *et al.*, 2019) includes worksheets that help the practitioner and parent gain a shared understanding of these factors. Filling out these worksheets is a bit like pulling apart an appliance on a kitchen table to see which wires are broken. If we can identify what's going wrong then the job is on, and we can start tinkering with changes. 'Don't skip through this part,' recommends Zoe, 'or it all comes crashing down because you won't know what to work on together!'

While identifying maintenance factors, be sensitive to a parent feeling blamed or inadequate. If we were making a cake, we'd be pouring in three cups of normalising into our bowl for every cup of psychoeducation. After all – what kind of parent wouldn't try to reassure a five-year-old that there aren't monsters under their bed, or feel hesitant about sending them to school when they've got an anxious stomach? These responses come from a place of love and protection – they're extremely well-intended.

As well as normalising, we can talk about child development processes and how we need to adapt our parenting as youngsters grow up.

'Children's needs change, and also their changing contexts require increasing amounts of independence,' says Vicki Curry. 'Parenting styles need to adapt to this and support them to build confidence.'

Above all, as Cathy Cresswell (Cresswell and Willetts, 2019) advises, parents shouldn't feel coerced – our main aim is to work alongside them, respectfully and with curiosity. As an aside, another excellent evidence-based approach which involves working directly with parents is Video Interaction Guidance (VIG). VIG practitioners are encouraged to model a hopefulness for positive change and a respect that parents are doing the best they can (Kennedy, Landor and Todd, 2011). These aren't bad philosophies for parent-led CBT, too. As Zoe suggests, 'While discussing maintenance factors, we can also ask about times when their children have coped with fears and done well, and point out examples of when parents have done things that have really helped them.'

USE EXAMPLES TO EXPLORE MAINTENANCE FACTORS IN ACTION

To help put potential maintenance factors into context, it's useful to give examples when talking with a parent. These can help normalise parenting styles and make maintenance factors feel less 'personal', thereby reducing the chance of a parent feeling like they're getting it all wrong.

To use the example from our case study, Bozena's instinct was to rush out and rescue Lena. This might have alleviated Bozena's own anxiety, but if Lena had ended up getting back in the car, she'd never have learnt that she could have coped with her feelings at football. This would have denied Lena an experience of coping. She'd also have learnt that football really is scary. It wouldn't be any surprise if Lena was even more anxious in future new situations.

Equally, Bozena might have never suggested football in the first place. She might be a really protective parent, keeping Lena back from taking part in sleepovers or going on school trips. This might stop Lena from developing her own sense of independence and confidence as she grows up. Again, we can wonder about this in a non-blaming way. Maybe Bozena was shy and hated sport at school. Why would she want her child to go through the same trauma? While done with good intentions, a parent's protectiveness and alertness might end up contributing to a child's heightened sense of anxiety, and if explained sensitively using examples parents might more naturally be inclined to think about anything they might unwittingly be doing that might lead to similar consequences.

An example of how parents can maintain a child's anxiety

Imagine it's a three-year-old's first day at a new nursery. He's understandably nervous and clings to his Mum's neck as they arrive. He's met his new nursery teacher before and seems to like her. The teacher gently suggests to his Mum that she says goodbye and leaves, but she's feeling really anxious, and can't bear to see her son like this. She decides it's all too much for him – he's too young – and they go back home to watch a movie, telling the teacher they'll try again tomorrow.

How do you think the boy will feel tomorrow morning when he's getting ready to leave for nursery again? Will his anxiety level be the same, lower or higher? What will he have learnt about himself, his fears and his ability to cope? What will he have learnt about his Mum's reaction to nursery as possibly being a place that he won't cope with, because his Mum brought him home?

If he doesn't make it in to nursery on the second day, how do you imagine the third day will go?

NORMALISE THAT WONDERING ABOUT ANXIOUS THOUGHTS CAN FEEL WEIRD

Bozena could have offered lots of reassurance, perhaps saying, 'You're going to be fine! There's nothing to worry about!' She might have also said, 'Don't be silly!'

When I recounted this as an example to a Mum I was working with, she exclaimed, 'And what's wrong with that!?'

She had a point. We need to pause at this moment and acknowledge that it feels so natural to reassure someone – only a sociopath who felt no empathy wouldn't have that instinct to want to make everything okay.

After acknowledging the humanity in it, we can then introduce the idea that too much reassurance can deny a child the chance to understand what they're scared of and can also feel dismissive to the child of the extent of their feelings.

Bozena could have asked, 'What's the worst thing about this – I know you're scared, but let's think...what are you really scared of?'

These kinds of questions don't exactly trip off the tongue – and its good practice to acknowledge that they can sound weird even to us, even when we're suggesting them. I once overhead a CWP say to a parent, 'I know, they're really awkward right – I find them hard myself!' She then got the parent involved in some role play so they could practise the kinds of conversations she might try to have with her child at home, which I thought was excellent practice.

Bozena's alternative questions could have helped Lena spot her anxious thoughts and start re-evaluating the truth of them. For example, if Lena was worried she'd feel like the odd one out, Mum could have reminded her of how she'd coped okay at her new school. They would have identified Lena's negative expectations and questioned them together, hopefully culminating in Lena feeling more inclined to 'give it a go' anyway.

FACING FEARS, AND MORE PSYCHOEDUCATION!

When we're working with parents we need to equip them with a good grasp of how facing fears helps, and why we need to drop safety behaviours. This is often the second lightbulb moment. If the parents get it and can tolerate their own anxiety while their child takes the steps, and the child feels motivated enough by the rewards on offer, then it stands a good chance of success.

Don't forget the detail. As Halldorsson *et al.* (2019) recommend, solid, well-thought-out plans will help parents feel confident about implementing the tasks at home without us. If a child is struggling to complete a step, we need to be on our toes with our problem-solving skills to work with the parents to make the step more manageable and ensure the reward is meaningful enough.

Often, parents feel more confident just by being given encouragement by a professional to 'go for it'. And, just like in any intervention, we need to keep checking they understand the rationale behind our suggestions – it's okay to ask directly, 'What do you think of this as an idea?' It's worth doing lots of this if a parent seems ambivalent, or is giving lots of 'maybe'-style answers to your questions, which can be a frustrating experience for the practitioner. We want our sessions to be useful – if we have any doubts that they're not being useful then we must be brave enough to ask the client what they think!

Vicki Curry's top tips around 'normalising' when talking about the model with parents

Because this model talks about the possible role of parents and others in a child's system in the development and maintenance of the child's anxiety, it is really important that practitioners explain it to parents in a way that doesn't make them feel blamed, guilty or judged.

One good way I have found of doing this is to provide psychoeducation that normalises the following:

- the existence of anxiety in children, and what they think/feel/do/what happens in their bodies when they are anxious

- the existence of anxiety in parents, and how they might behave when their child seems anxious

- the links between the two.

Here are some ways of talking to parents that I have found helpful over the years.

1. Say: 'As parents, we are designed to protect our children – it's in our bones to want to do so.' Sometimes I illustrate this by talking about how animals behave in nature documentaries when they are looking out for and protecting their young.

2. Say: 'As parents, we look out for signs of danger and will step in to protect our children at all costs – particularly if they seem vulnerable to us in some way. These are very primal urges. No one likes seeing a child – let alone their own child – in distress. Resisting the pull to step in and help them out can be really difficult at times.'

3. I often play parents a clip from *Finding Nemo* ('Nemo goes to school' – available on YouTube). This is a two-minute clip

of Nemo and his dad getting ready for Nemo's first day at school. It is a great example because Nemo's dad is a loving parent who has a great relationship with his son; and if you remember the story, there are very good reasons why he might be particularly primed to worry about Nemo. I ask parents to watch the clip, and to think about more and less helpful things that Nemo's dad does to support him. It's a humorous clip that usually makes parents smile – but also makes them think about ways we sometimes behave when we are a bit anxious about our children doing something new that – particularly if our children have a tendency towards anxiety (which Nemo doesn't) – might end up with them feeling a bit worried too!

4. Emphasise it's not just parents: children learn from watching others and others are protective too (grandparents, cousins, friends and teachers).

5. Say: 'You're really good at supporting him when he's anxious and helping him feel okay. As children get older they have to do more things by themselves – learn to be more independent. So we need to think how we can teach him all those things that you're really good at doing, so he can do them himself when you're not there.'

6. It can be helpful for parents when practitioners give low-level examples of anxiety they might have experienced and how that affected things for them and their interactions with children – perhaps as a babysitter, teaching assistant or even as a parent. Make sure you don't talk about anything too hectic though – think about what it would be like for parents to hear and discuss your ideas with your supervisor. If you don't want to talk about yourself, you can give common examples of everyday things parents do to illustrate the model, such as saying 'be careful', asking 'are you feeling okay?', or saying 'are you sure?' when their child says they want to do something new.

7. Explain that it's totally normal and completely appropriate and helpful for parents to offer some reassurance and encouragement to their children, such as when they try new things, like saying 'It will be great' or 'You'll be fine' if they're a bit nervous about saying their line in an assembly. It can also be a quick fix in calming down an anxious child. However, we aren't always there to provide this reassurance and sometimes we overdo it. The more children are given reassurance by others, the more they'll likely think they need it. This can get in the way of them learning to become more independent and confident by themselves and can keep their anxiety going. So children also need to learn to reassure themselves as they get older.

TAKE-AWAYS

► Working with parents makes sense given what we know about the maintenance factors involved in child anxiety.

► Parenting is a tough job, and no one ever gets it 100 per cent right – and nor should they as that would totally mess up a child!

► What helps in practice when working with parents is lots of encouragement, psychoeducation, normalising, and using metaphors and examples.

► If you're working from the therapist manual and things get stuck, then Creswell *et al.*'s *Parent-Led CBT for Child Anxiety* (2017) has lots of fantastic ideas on how to overcome common stumbling blocks.

► Acknowledging the weirdness in trying new approaches is important – and role plays can help with this.

► Don't forget how important it is to get a parent on board with helping their child work through feared steps – and try to make them feel really supported by helping them develop a solid plan for them to try out.

CHAPTER 20

Coping Strategies, Problem Solving and Relaxation Activities

Coping strategies, problem solving and relaxation activities are all important aspects of wellbeing work – but it's important to grasp the subtle distinctions between them and understand what works best, and when.

THIS CHAPTER WILL COVER:

- Coping strategies and tools that help young people in the heat of the moment
- Why problem solving is a useful skill for young people to learn
- How relaxation activities can help young people self-regulate their emotions through often-stressful school years

---

COPING STRATEGIES AND TOOLS

Coping strategies are tools and techniques that young people can use as they tackle their difficulties step by step. In psychology, coping is defined as 'conscious volitional efforts to regulate emotion, cognition, behavior, physiology, and the environment in response to stressful events or circumstances' (Compas *et al.*, 2001, p.89).

It can be useful to think of coping tools as being like the walking aids and other apparatus that physiotherapists recommend for rehabilitation. During the first Covid pandemic, children's author Michael Rosen spent a month in intensive care and had to learn to walk again. Michael was first taught to use a Zimmer frame – and thought he'd never manage without one. He then progressed to two walking sticks, which he found really hard to give up – and finally just used a single stick (which he affectionately named 'stickymcstickface'). Eventually, Michael managed to shuffle from his bed to the toilet and back unaided, remembering the encouraging words of his physio and singing M People's 'Search for the hero' to himself as he went. The Zimmer frame, walking sticks and mental self-talk were Michael's coping tools and techniques which helped him progress through his recovery steps one at a time.

Just like physiotherapists, we can think with our young people about what coping tools will help them each stage of the way – all the while mindful that they'll need to drop each one eventually to achieve their full 'recovery'. So, if our client's anxiety goes through the roof during class because they're worried their teacher is going to ask them a question, then we might teach them a coping skill like a positive self-talk phrase while staying engaged with the lesson and open to the possibility of being asked something. Keeping their head down or making an excuse and going to the toilet would of course not be coping tools – they're safety behaviours. So – when thinking about the following coping strategies and tools, always apply them knowing they're a temporary aid and not a permanent solution.

▧ TRY IT OUT: coping tools or safety behaviours

Can you think of a situation where you regularly feel anxious, or used to feel anxious? It might be a work thing, like having to make presentations – or it might be about meeting new people in social situations. Can you reflect on any helpful coping tools that you used to use but no longer need, or any safety behaviours that might still be knocking about and potentially holding you back?

FACE

FACE is a sequential set of practical steps that helps pull us back from a sense of overwhelm when we're facing a strong emotional response to a situation – particularly if we're feeling out of control. It was invented by Russ Harris, one of the proponents of acceptance and commitment therapy. The steps are:

Focus on what's in your control

Acknowledge your thoughts and feelings

Come back into your body

Engage in what you're doing

The 'doughnut of control' (Chapter 18) can help us suss out what's in and out of our direct control, and we can use some of the other coping skills below to help us get back into our bodies and out of our heads.

Tense and relax

When we experience strong emotions we tend to tense our muscles. Tensing and then relaxing them helps shift our focus of attention from our minds back into our bodies – the 'coming back into the body' third FACE step. The nice thing about 'tense and relax' exercises is that they can be done anywhere fairly unobtrusively, just using your hands or your feet. For example, you could try the following:

1. Put your focus in your hands and feet.

2. Feel your feet on the floor and scrunch your toes like you're a bird gripping onto a branch, then release.

3. Make your fists into balls and then relax them.

4. If you're sitting on a chair, place your palms on the seat and try to lift your body up an inch or two, then gently release and roll your shoulders a little.

Cold water

Splashing cold water on your face is a great way of quickly reducing a strong emotion. Just run a cold tap and splash water on your face – or dip your face into a bowl full of cold water for five seconds. All mammals have a 'dive reflex' and putting your face in cold water helps activate this, turning on your parasympathetic nervous system temporarily. You then need to re-engage in whatever you're doing next as soon as you can.

5-4-3-2-1

This technique gets us re-engaging all our senses to help ground ourselves. Look for five things you see around you, four things you can touch or feel, three things you can hear, two things you can smell and one thing you can taste. When you're feeling strong emotions it can be hard to remember which sense comes first, so it's worth practising it live in sessions – don't rush through it. Spend some time on it and recap on the exercise again at the end of the session.

Coping cards

Coping cards and coping statements can help your client get through a difficult time by reminding them of their strengths or helping to reframe a situation. Young people can store them on their phones as images or notes, or carry them on small cards in their pocket. They're not 'positive self-affirmations' that are going to radically transform our lives – sorry, there's not much evidence they work like that – they're just small helpers along the way. Spend some time helping your client write down the statements that mean the most to them – or even offer to record voice memos with them. Here are some possibilities:

> *This fear is from last year.*
>
> *Thoughts aren't facts…I don't need to believe everything that pops into my mind.*
>
> *I can do this.*
>
> *I'm okay just as I am.*
>
> *If I feel down, I can remind myself it's only emotions – it will pass.*
>
> *This is just a feeling. I've followed this feeling in the past. Now I'm going to follow my plan, and not this old feeling.*

Apps

The NHS has a list of recommended mental health apps for young people and children. Some are great as 'go-to' resources in times of difficulty, including grounding and distraction strategies. Others include daily motivational tips and discussion forums. Some apps also help with graded exposure and behavioural activation activity scheduling, including planning tools and reminders. Lots of apps are going through trials for effectiveness at the time of writing – search 'NHS self-help apps' and ask young people what works best for them so you can pass on recommendations to others.

Problem solving

Problem solving is an intervention in its own right in the world of adult low intensity work, and it's supported by strong evidence for its effectiveness (Mynors-Wallis and Lau, 2010). We can use problem solving to help clients identify and overcome practical issues that are affecting their wellbeing – such as applying for a college place. Problem solving can also help when planning steps in depression and anxiety interventions. If we were to use the spaceship metaphor in Chapter 15, problems are like the asteroid belts that get in the way of our client's rocket as it blasts towards its goal. When we identify a problem, we can either solve it, try to feel better about it, learn to tolerate it or stay miserable – it's our choice! If we want to learn to solve it, then the following steps are useful.

Step 1: Identify the problem.

Step 2: Think through two or three different possible solutions.

Step 3: Work out the pros and cons of each.

Step 4: Choose a solution and make a plan – what, where, when, with whom?

Step 5: Do it! Then review it – did it work?

Check out the example of a problem-solving worksheet below, developed as our client Sadiqa works towards her goal of overcoming her vomit phobia. Always remember to check in with how the week's plan went in the following session, and if needed, think of different solutions until you find one that works. People who learn to problem solve are better equipped to deal with the inevitable challenges of life, and once equipped with this skill the hope is a young person will improve their view of themselves, too – as someone who's resilient and capable.

Sadiqa's problem-solving worksheet

What's the mission?

To eat dinner downstairs with Mum as a step towards my goal of going to the restaurant for George's party in three weeks' time.

What's the problem?

I'll feel really sick and anxious about being sick or Mum being sick.

Possible solutions	Advantages	Disadvantages
Leave the room	Won't feel sick any more	Won't help me in the long run
Use a coping card on my phone	I might be able to complete the step and stay there	I'll still feel sick!
Eat with my eyes closed	I'll still achieve the step and I could try to eat with my eyes open the next time	I'll still be able to hear Mum eat

Which solution will you choose to try?
I'm going to eat with my eyes closed.

What will you do, and when?
Tomorrow, I'm going to tell Mum I'm going to be eating with her but that I'll do it with my eyes closed. I'm going to ask her to keep telling me I'm doing well, and remind me it's just a feeling, and I'm going to stay and eat dinner with her for at least 15 minutes.

How did it go?

RELAXATION ACTIVITIES

As neuroscientist Dean Burnett (2019) points out, adults can really do young people a disservice when they don't acknowledge just how stressful school life and adolescence can be. And an important part of our work is to help young people learn to regulate themselves so they can ameliorate the effects of various daily stresses.

Emotional regulation is a broader term than coping – there are overlaps – but in the context of low intensity work, it involves helping clients identify things that they do that relax and calm them. By reconnecting with the parasympathetic nervous system, they can help their minds and bodies remember feelings of peace.

Some relaxation activities can also be used as coping tools, but they should be integrated and practised, regardless of how our clients feel. Unlike coping tools they don't need to be slowly dropped as our resilience improves. With only eight sessions, it can be hard for us as practitioners to ascertain whether a relaxation activity is becoming a safety behaviour, so we need to stay alert to any a danger of them becoming ways of avoiding difficult emotions, which means they won't be helpful in the long run.

About five years ago I started working in a new school and I'd often arrive feeling anxious. When I felt like this I'd do a five-minute mindfulness exercise in my car which would calm me down a little. I started doing these more and more often, but after a few weeks I noticed I was arriving feeling anxious every single morning. It was as if the practice was fuelling anticipatory anxiety, rather than diminishing it. My relaxation activity had effectively become a safety behaviour.

Progressive muscle relaxation

Progressive muscle relaxation is a deep relaxation technique that involves tensing and then relaxing your muscles from top to toe. It's great to do in the evening, lying on your bed. There are plenty of five- to ten-minute audio recordings online to follow – have a search or find a script and record one yourself while reading it to your client in the session so they can take it away and use it themselves.

Listening to music

This is an excellent exercise in training our minds to focus externally. Close your eyes, play your favourite music track and put all your attention into the sounds. What different instruments can you hear being played? How many singers are there? Are there any sound effects going on?

Finger breathing

Many young people struggle with 'follow-your-breath' mindfulness practices. These can heighten their focus internally in the chest and belly areas where difficult anxiety sensations are often felt. Finger breathing keeps two other senses at play – touch and sight – so it's more involving and less internally focused. Here's how to do it. Stretch out your left hand. Use your right hand's index finger as a pointer and run it up the side of your little finger as you breathe in through your nose. Slide down the other side as you breathe out through your mouth. Keep going, traversing the valleys and peaks of your fingers, till you reach the thumb, then reverse!

Square breathing (or box breathing)

Square breathing helps breath regulation and can induce a state of calm. Find a square-shaped thing near you – it could be your phone, a window, a book – whatever. Breathe in slowly while counting one, two, three, four seconds as you go up one side of the square. Hold your breath for a count of four as you go along the top horizontal line of the square. Gently exhale for a count of four as you go down the other side. Then hold the count for four as you go along the bottom side. And repeat!

Rest your head

Why not try this now, if you're sitting at a desk? Just stop what you're doing and rest your head on your folded arms on the desk. Close your eyes, relax your neck, breathe out deeply and just let the desk take the full weight of the heaviest part of your body. Notice where the warmth of the breath reaches your skin. Smell the wood or glass of the desk. Do nothing. Just relax!

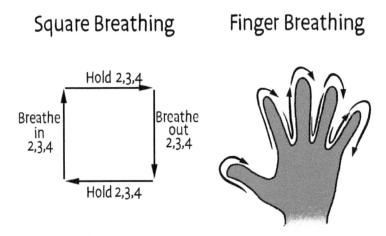

Figure 20.1: Square breathing and finger breathing

Whatever works

Try to help identify whatever works for your client – whether it's taking a bath, lighting a candle, reading, going for a run, chatting with friends, praying, gaming, connecting with an LGBTQ+ network online, being outside in the woods or a park... Whatever works, the important thing is to encourage them to integrate it as an important part of their day to help them rest and recharge. If the activities are linked to their personal values, even better.

TAKE-AWAYS

► Problem solving is a really useful life skill for young people to learn. It can help overcome road-blocks during interventions for anxiety and depression, and if learnt well it can enhance a young person's sense of agency, too.

► Coping tools and strategies are temporary aids to help clients work through the steps in their intervention plan and deal with strong emotional difficulties.

► Relaxation activities are so important given many young people's experience of stress at school and home. They can be built into a client's life to help them relax and regulate their emotions, but as a rule, relaxation activities should not be regularly used as coping tools – otherwise they might become safety behaviours.

CHAPTER 21

A Brief Overview of More Complex Needs

Low intensity CBT practitioners focus mainly on anxiety and low mood, but it's useful to have some understanding of other difficulties which may need additional assessment and treatment. It's also important to hold neurodiversity in mind so that we can adapt interventions and consider whether a young person might benefit from further support.

THIS CHAPTER COVERS:

- Neurodiversity: the basics with ASC and ADHD
- Some of the signs of obsessive-compulsive disorder
- Questions to ask if you're considering post-traumatic stress disorder
- Things to consider with eating disorders
- What to do when both anxiety and low mood are present

THE POWER OF WORDS

First, if we're considering the value of further assessment, it's worth being extra cautious around the words we use. When wearing a 'mental health professional' hat, take care with using labels or making definite statements – these can quickly be interpreted as diagnoses which we're not qualified to offer. For example, it's much better to say, 'I'm wondering if you'd benefit from some further support to help you with your eating issues,' rather than, 'I'm thinking you could benefit from assessment for Anorexia.'

NEURODIVERSITY

We're all wired differently, and 'neurodiversity' is a nice way of phrasing that. Within a broad spectrum of differences, autistic spectrum condition (ASC) and attention deficit hyperactivity disorder (ADHD) are two diagnoses that attract lively debate. With relevant training, neither of these should preclude us from working with young people. But what are they, in a nutshell?

The NICE website gives some good guidance on identifying ASC, but very briefly, ASC can give rise to difficulties with communication, social interaction and interacting with others. First – and do ask your client how they like to describe themselves before using labels – an autistic person might lack flexible social imaginative play and creativity, have strong particular interests and have a rigid set of repetitive behaviours. Routine can be really important – and changes to timetables can be very challenging.

If you think a young person has ASC, chat it through with your supervisor. There are ways of tailoring interventions that might be worth exploring – as is the idea of further assessment.

When working with someone with a diagnosis, take care not to over-attribute difficulties to 'just being ASC' – this is known as 'diagnostic overshadowing'. Low mood and anxiety are more common in neurodivergent than neurotypical young people.

ADHD is a diagnosis that describes a difficulty in focusing attention on one task at a time, along with impulsivity and hyperactivity (NICE, 2018).

One person describes her experience of having ADHD like this: 'Imagine a brass band following you about, playing loudly, and then trying to get some work done. You would forget things, not listen, and make mistakes too!' (Lister, 2020).

Again, ADHD symptoms should be no barrier for someone getting help, but it will be worth thinking with your supervisor about adapting the intervention or considering making a referral for further assessment.

OBSESSIVE COMPULSIVE DISORDER (OCD)

OCD is 'characterised by the presence of either obsessions or compulsions, but commonly both' (NICE, 2005). An obsession is defined as an unwanted intrusive thought, image or urge that repeatedly enters the person's mind. Compulsions are repetitive behaviours or mental acts that the person feels driven to perform. A compulsion can either be overt and observable by others, such as checking that a door is locked, or a covert mental act that cannot be observed, such as repeating a certain phrase in one's mind.

The RCADS outcome measures include scoring for OCD, and this can be a helpful first indication that the problem might be more complex than a simpler form of anxiety.

It's quite common for OCD sufferers to experience troubling thoughts about being their worst nightmare – a paedophile or murderer, for example – or to have intrusive thoughts about causing significant harm to others. So it's worth being aware that OCD can involve a huge sense of shame for a young person when gently exploring it as a possibility. Out of respect to OCD sufferers, we should never say anyone's 'a little bit OCD'. It's a commonly misunderstood condition that causes huge distress and impairment. It's not about keeping your books nicely lined up – it's about living with a monster that urges you to do things or else your worst fears will come true.

It's likely that low intensity practitioners would refer someone with possible OCD to a more specialist CAMHS service for assessment or treatment.

PTSD AND C-PTSD

People can experience post-traumatic stress disorder (PTSD) and complex post-traumatic stress disorder (C-PTSD) when memories aren't processed properly following one or more traumatic events that typically involve a sense of extreme danger or threat.

PTSD can occur after a single-event trauma, whereas C-PTSD can result from multiple traumas. Symptoms include avoiding reminders of the trauma, hyper-arousal, emotional numbing, flashbacks and nightmares, emotional dysregulation, problems with relationships, negative self-perceptions and lowered mood. The young person may also be dissociating – feeling out of touch with themselves or what's around them.

It's worth remembering that not everyone who experiences a traumatic event suffers PTSD afterwards and concerned parents and teachers may often want help for young people when they've actually processed what's happened and are coping okay. But always be alert to signs of PTSD – for example, if helping with sleep hygiene, be mindful of particularly intrusive, repetitive nightmares.

If you are wondering about PTSD, some useful questions to ask include:

> 'Have you ever experienced a difficult event in your life which still significantly affects you now?'

> 'Do the memories come back frequently, without warning, causing strong emotions?'

> 'Is this a problem that you want help with now?'

According to current NICE guidance, both PTSD and C-PTSD are best treated using trauma-focused CBT, or EMDR (eye movement desensitisation and reprocessing).

EATING DISORDERS

If you have concerns around dieting or restrictive eating, weight loss, attitudes around weight or shape, or other red flags as listed on the NICE website then do talk with the young person about these and consider referring to the school nurse or a CAMHS professional. As NICE guidance states, be mindful that the young person may well find it distressing to talk about any eating issues – and parents and carers can have strong reactions too, so proceed with sensitivity, and of course talk with your supervisor about the best tack to take.

Eating disorders are generally treated by Specialist CAMHS services, who offer a range of interventions including family therapy and specially adapted CBT.

▨ TRY IT OUT: learn more about eating disorders

You'll notice the section on eating disorders is a little shorter than others. Get yourself onto the NICE website and start researching the different kinds of eating disorders and the latest advice on how to spot them and help people with them. If you're familiar with the NICE site you'll be better placed to signpost young people, professionals and parents and carers to the right kind of help according to the latest clinical guidance.

CO-MORBID ANXIETY AND DEPRESSION

Researchers have concluded it's quite common for young people to experience both depression and anxiety at the same time (Melton *et al.*, 2016). As Fuggle *et al.* (2012) point out, it's no wonder that having one difficulty increases the chance of having another. If you're missing school because you're anxious, then you might start missing your friends and fall behind in your work, and this may well lead to you feeling depressed. As mentioned in Chapter 6, it's important to get as good a sense as possible during assessment of what the primary difficulty is, and this might take extra time.

We would then offer the treatment for the primary difficulty. In low intensity work we don't want to be using two different manuals simultaneously or chopping and changing between sessions. The danger with this is it dilutes the main treatment and worsens the chances of success (Whittington and Grey, 2014). Instead, the hope is that by helping with one issue, we will also help alleviate the other. And thankfully, there are aspects of graded exposure that cross over with behavioural activation, and vice versa, and some of the activities could be tweaked slightly to be more helpful. For example, if building a graded exposure ladder with a young person who is also feeling low, we could think about including activities that not only help them face their fears but also, in time, will lead to a greater sense of pleasure and achievement. As Whittington suggests, it's better to normalise the fact that anxiety can get in the way of treating depression, and vice versa, but keep our focus on the main intervention.

TAKE-AWAYS

► As an EMHP or CWP, you're on the frontline and will come across many different presentations – it's not your job to diagnose these, but it helps to have some awareness of them so you can help signpost or think about further help.

► We should aim to offer excellent interventions to neurotypical and atypical clients alike and should use supervision and training to further develop our skills – or refer on if we don't feel skilled enough.

► Be mindful of PTSD symptoms and ask appropriate questions if you suspect they might be present.

► OCD is characterised by someone having repeated compulsions or obsessive thoughts – and often having both.

► Eating disorders are increasing, and we need to work with other professionals including school nurses and eating disorder services to ensure a young person is properly assessed.

► It's common for both anxiety and low mood to be present simultaneously. If it gets complex, keep it simple, and ask for the client's lead on what they want help with most. Aim to treat one thing properly rather than two things half-heartedly!

CHAPTER 22

Blueprinting and Endings

Hopefully our clients will have learnt a few life skills in their time with us. When we come to wrap things up, it's important to help them identify what's been helpful and what they need to do to keep moving forward.

THIS CHAPTER COVERS:

- How and when to talk about the ending
- A technique to help a client remember what they need to keep up with to maintain progress
- How to write a closing letter

When finishing up a piece of work with a client, it's important to praise the hard work they've put in, review what they've learnt and what they need to keep doing, and also to acknowledge how they feel about the sessions ending. It's tempting to avoid all this, but it's an elephant in the room if you don't address it! It can be hard to say goodbye – both for the client and practitioner. So don't leave it till the last moment. Make sure your client knows how many sessions you have booked in right from session zero, and consider saying, 'We've got three more sessions after this one' when you're halfway through the intervention to start to help the client get used to the fact it'll be wrapping up. Some clients worry they won't be able to cope on their own or won't have access to support. It can be helpful to normalise this by verbalising it, but also encouraging them to think positively about what they've learnt through the intervention – and also reminding them of the strengths and personal qualities you've noticed them develop, too.

When wrapping up, it's useful to pull out the back-up team drawing to help your client think about ongoing support. You could also encourage your client to think about their top take-aways from the sessions, write out new coping card statements, or start making a 'virtual resource box' of things they'll find helpful (such as a music playlist, different activities, positive voice memos on their phone and so on). Perhaps also think with them of a way of celebrating the last session.

DRAWING A WIND TURBINE OR VIRTUOUS FLOWER

This exercise (see Figure 22.1) can help a client to summarise the key changes they've made and what they need to keep doing to maintain progress. The first step is to ask your client to think of a positive new belief about themselves in relation to the problem they've been working on. They don't have to completely buy this new belief, but it's got to be the opposite of how they felt when they came in for help. You then start thinking with them about what positive things they need to keep doing, and – crucially – how these things will help build this new sense of themselves.

It's the opposite of a 'vicious flower' (Moorey, 2010) which highlights an unhelpful self-belief and the mechanisms that keep that belief going, prolonging the difficulty. What I really like about the exercise is the subtle but powerful way it shows how behavioural change leads to positive consequences.

Here's a vignette that describes how to draw one with a client.

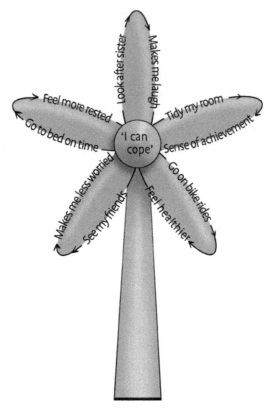

Figure 22.1: A 'virtuous flower' or 'wind turbine' exercise can help a client identify what actions are going to power them forward to reinforce their new belief about themselves

Drawing a wind turbine

1. I remember when we first met you had a view of yourself – you often said you thought that you'd always feel a certain way (e.g. 'I won't be able to cope'). What would you like your new belief to be about yourself? It could be something we've started working towards that you'd like to continue with so it doesn't matter if you don't believe it's 100 per cent true.

2. Write this as an 'I am' or 'I can' statement down in the middle of a sheet of paper and draw a circle around it. For example, 'I can cope with my exams' or 'I can manage my moods'.

3. Okay, imagine this is a wind turbine and the wind blades are the things you've learnt that help. Each blade represents an action that's important to keep doing to keep reinforcing this new belief about yourself.

4. Let's now think about some of the things you've learnt and are doing differently since we first met. What comes to mind? Shall we look back through the worksheets too?

5. Let's write each action down on an edge of each wind blade, and then think after each one about how that reinforces your belief and helps, and write that on the other side of the blade. For example, 'I can plan to see or talk to friends each day' is something you can do, and this helps because 'being sociable lifts my mood'.

6. That's great – what do you make of this? Would it be helpful to take a picture of this on your phone as a reminder of what can help?

7. How about we have a final check-in session in X weeks' time to check these are still helpful?

Table 22.1: A blueprinting template

Moving On Up – My Blueprint
The problem I came for help with was...
What I know was keeping the problem going was...
The things I've found most helpful over the weeks have been...
I know I need to keep doing the following for my own wellbeing...
I'll notice if things start to go wrong because...

The people or things that would help if things do go wrong are…
My goals for the future are…

WRITING A BLUEPRINT SHEET

You could structure the blueprinting a bit more formally by using a 'blueprint' or 'relapse prevention sheet' – your service might provide you with one (similar to Table 22.1). If not, just make one up using the same or similar questions.

WRITING A CLOSING LETTER

A closing letter is something physical that a young person or family can keep as a reminder of your work with them. It shows you've spent extra time thinking about them. When writing it, steer clear of technical language like 'formulation' and 'maintenance factors' that might get in the way of your client understanding things clearly. Instead of a letter you could always make them a short video or audio recording of you telling them these things. Hopefully it'll give them a nice warm glow while also giving them practical reminders of what they've learnt and a summary of changes they've made. A good 'strengths-based' letter should include:

- things you've enjoyed while working with them

- a summary of the problems that brought them to the intervention

- an explanation as to what you agreed was keeping the difficulty going

- the steps you took together to make things better

- some positive qualities and changes you've noticed while with them

- reminders about what you both think will be helpful going forward.

Francesca Cicconi, clinical lead at an NHS wellbeing service, suggests that we read the letter out loud to our client in our final session and then hand it to them, rather than sending it in the post. This way you can get their feedback and make changes, and it'll also likely have a stronger emotional resonance if delivered in person. If it's been a really involved piece of work, you could even consider reading it out in the penultimate session and revisiting it in the final one. Always be transparent about who will receive a copy of the letter (sometimes GPs are copied in automatically), and if a copy will be stored by your service.

BOOKING IN A REVIEW SESSION

If at all possible it can be helpful to book in a review session two or three months after the intervention ends. This can help the client hold in mind the things they need to keep doing, knowing they'll be checked in on at a date in the future. You can also revisit the blueprint and make changes at that session.

A sample closing letter

Dear Louis,

I've really enjoyed working with you over the past eight weeks and I wanted to write to you to sum up some of the things we've done and what could be helpful going forwards.

We first met because your Mum was worried about you having a low mood, and you agreed that you were feeling down. I was really impressed with your openness and honesty right from that first session. You set a goal of getting out of your house more often and reconnecting with friends. We thought together about how staying in and avoiding friends kind of worked for a bit, but then it became like the depression was this huge giant locking you in and winning, and it wasn't helping in the long run.

Over the next few weeks, your determination was remarkable. Depression is no fun at all, and it wasn't easy for you to talk about how it had started, and how you felt like you'd be a burden for talking about it. Hopefully you have now changed your mind about that, and I know you'd be an amazing support to any of your friends going through the same thing.

It was fascinating to hear you talk about all the things that really matter to you – being kind to people, spending time running and staying fit, and getting pleasure out of cooking for others, among other things.

While trying to get going with the different activities we set you up to try, you said your phone reminder to 'follow the plan, not the mood' was helpful. That's something that'll be important to remember. You also said it was useful to try to understand when your mind was in a spin, going over and over things, and to notice when it was happening and go and make a cup of tea or do something active, put your mind elsewhere.

You've worked really hard, and you should feel proud of the progress you've made. I know you didn't quite make your third goal of being back in school full time, but you're getting there. You also know that you can talk to your dad and friend Jack if your mood dips, and also use the apps we installed on your phone.

It was a pleasure working with you, and next session let's look at what's going to be helpful for you going forwards – we can write up a short list together, maybe if helpful?

All the best,
Amelie

TAKE-AWAYS

▶ Endings can generate feelings for client and practitioner: it's okay to acknowledge and normalise that a client will have these too.

▶ A 'virtuous flower' or 'wind turbine' helps capture the things a client has learnt to do and needs to keep going with as they move towards more firmly embracing a positive belief about themselves.

▶ Closing letters can be very powerful: consider writing one and reading it to the client in the final or penultimate session to allow them a chance to reflect on it with you.

CHAPTER 23

What to Do When Things Get Stuck

When we put our heart and soul into preparing and then running a session it can be really demoralising if it doesn't go well. And it's going to happen – very little in life gets easily resolved in a nice, neat bow and in mental health there are always frayed ends. It's important to acknowledge when things aren't going well and then have a plan as to what to do next – here are some ideas on how to do just that.

THIS CHAPTER COVERS:

- How to stay mindful of our own responses when things aren't working out

- Some questions that can help us address potential issues with our client

- The value of motivational interviewing

- How to help clients see the value of home practice tasks

- What to do when things get worse

ISSUES WITH LOW MOTIVATION

When working with a young person who doesn't seem bothered about trying out the things you both agree might help, you might feel like tearing your hair out and screaming, 'But we've still got 50 pages of the manual to get through!'

There are usually good reasons for low motivation levels. If you've had counselling before and it hasn't helped or you've had a poor experience with a social worker, you might not welcome support from yet another professional with open arms. When a 15-year-old arrives for his session ten minutes late, shrugs his shoulders and tells you he doesn't see the point in being there, it's so easy just to see it as 'typical teenage behaviour', but it's essential we look into it further before trying to move on.

Try to recognise but then bracket any feelings of annoyance you might have and go into curiosity mode. When exploring what looks like low motivation, we might ask some open questions like these:

'How are you feeling about trying to make these changes?'

'Have you had any experiences with professionals like me that might be putting you off?'

'Am I getting things wrong here? Are there things I could be doing to make these sessions better and more useful for you?'

'How powered up are you to work on this at the moment – what's your battery level like?' (using Figure 23.1)

Figure 23.1: Battery levels are a useful way of gauging levels of motivation and energy

If we're encountering resistance to our work then try to 'roll with it' rather than challenge it, as Paul Stallard puts it (2005). It's a bit like standing side-on and wondering what's going on rather than grappling with someone from the front. And of course, asking 'Why are you not taking this seriously?' is not going to go down well!

A lot of teens feel misunderstood as it is – I did, and I'm sure you did too. But that's hard to remember when we've got a job to do. As Vicki Curry says, 'When time is short and we're fixated on fixing a problem, we can fall into a trap of trying to persuade someone to think, or feel, or behave differently.'

This can set up an unhelpful dynamic, where the more steps forward we take, the further our client retreats. If we fall into this rut, it's important to have the patience and curiosity to investigate what's really going on for our client. This is where 'motivational interviewing' comes to the fore.

MOTIVATIONAL INTERVIEWING

Motivational interviewing is about rolling with the resistance – taking it seriously and trying to open up an exploration. It requires a Socratic stance. Get back into 'bumbling detective' mode and ask the young person if it's okay to explore things further. After all, you want to make the sessions useful – and this matters.

A great way to follow the process of motivational interviewing is by drawing out a grid on a piece of A4 paper (see Table 23.1), and titling it 'My decision grid' – to help ensure the young person sees it as their decision, not yours! You should then have four boxes. Write 'staying the same' at the top of the left column, and 'changing things up' above the right column. You can then mark the top row as 'positives' and the bottom row as 'negatives.'

Taking each box in turn, ask the young person about what they see as the positives and negatives of things staying the same, and the pros and cons of trying to change. It's a nice exercise in equality and demonstrates respectfulness – remembering throughout that it's ultimately their call, not yours. Of course, you can work actively to open things out – asking for example for any positives or negatives in a year's time, and you could also help them try to sum things up by getting them to circle the most important pros and cons. It's then about seeing how these factors play into the work and their goals and tweaking the intervention to suit. For example, if one of the negatives for change is that 'the facing fear steps are really scary', then that's important information, and you might consider making the steps more accessible.

Of course, some young people might struggle to write down any pros for making changes. At least now you have a solid understanding of that and can discuss it with your supervisor. An intervention may well be futile if there really isn't any motivation to engage. This kind of honest 'grasping the nettle' endeavour can save hours and hours of frustration that can result from an elephant in the room not being discussed.

✱ **Table 23.1: A decision grid for motivational interviewing**

My decision grid

Staying the same - Positives	Changing things up - Positives
Staying the same - Negatives	Changing things up - Negatives

▦ TRY IT OUT: motivational interviewing grid

Draw out a grid for yourself and think about something you're strug-gling to do that you know you probably should (perhaps like trying to do more exercise or going to bed earlier). Stick down the pros and cons into each box, following the guide. Then review the lists and ask yourself if the benefits of making the change outweigh the negatives. Are there enough reasons to 'go for it'?

BETWEEN-SESSION TASKS

In Chapter 4 I suggested you try to carve out 20 minutes a day to do something nice and replenishing for yourself over the following week. How did it go? Honestly? It probably won't be a surprise to hear it's very rare for anyone to complete this task! In my time tutoring, a very few trainees have managed it three or four days a week. A lot haven't managed it even once!

My behavioural activation teacher Peter Garwood encouraged us to do the same exercise when I was in training. We returned the following week and, like all good CBT therapists should, Peter asked us how the home practice had gone. We all meekly admitted we hadn't managed to complete it.

Peter asked us, 'So, you all agreed last week that it'd be a valuable thing to do, right?'

And we nodded in agreement. Yes, we had.

'And you understood that the research shows that it's really important to do these tasks for improvement to happen?'

We nodded again.

'Yet you still didn't do them?'

Umm-hum. We nodded some more.

'So, I guess in a way – and I don't mean this harshly – but thinking it was a useful exercise to try, and knowing that it's the between-session stuff that counts... I guess it's kind of a waste of your own time coming back today, isn't it?'

We nodded again.

'And it's kind of wasting my time too!'

I'd never recommend this style of conversation with a client – and nor would Peter – but it's always stuck in my mind! Through this exchange, Peter demonstrated so clearly that the ultimate responsibility for change is with the client – not the therapist. No elephants in the room with Peter Garwood, clearly.

Anyhow – back to it. What helps when it comes to getting home practice tasks done?

First, consider calling them 'action steps', 'experiments' or 'positive changes' rather than home practice – and definitely don't call it homework. Most young people definitely have enough of that already! EMHP Suzanne Everill suggests we call it 'in-between session wellbeing work', which gives it a nice positive framing.

Second, when discussing next week's home practice tasks, really check out your client's take on them. Do they see the point of them? Do they make sense? How might they be helpful? Who could help you do them? When will you do them? If they can't see any rhyme or reason for trying them out, or have no idea how they'll fit them into their lives, they're very unlikely to happen. Be active and help your client problem solve any difficulties that might get in the way and think together about solutions.

Christine Padesky (2020a) suggests asking questions like 'And what could get in the way of you doing these things this week?' and 'How would you like to handle that?'

The last home practice task I encouraged a group of trainees to do was a total flop. Their feedback the following week was that I should have given a clearer example of the task during the session, perhaps demonstrating it live. They said it would also have helped if I'd asked them to grab their phones and set daily reminders for the following week. Fail to plan and plan to fail, as the saying goes!

A conversation about between-session tasks

Practitioner: To help improve your mood we've come up with an idea for you to meet up with two different friends – one on Saturday and one on Sunday. It looks like it'll take a bit of effort to put the plan in place, so I just want to check if you think it's worth it?

Client: Yeah, I think it's worth giving it a go.

Practitioner: And this might sound like a silly question, but why do you think it's worth the effort, for you?

Client: Because actually I really want to get out and see my friends. I miss them, especially now the weather's getting nicer. I think it'll give me a boost.

Practitioner: It sounds like it is really important for you. Just thinking ahead though, what could get in the way of you doing these things?

Client: Well, if I don't get around to texting them, or they don't text me back.

Practitioner: Yes – that might be an issue. How could we think as to how we make sure you remember to text them – when would you do it? And what would you do if they didn't text back?

Client: I guess I could set a reminder on my phone to text them after school.

Practitioner: What time would you set the reminder for?

Client: About 5 pm I think.

Practitioner: And if you didn't get a response, what would you do next?

Client: I could always send another message or try the group chat to see if anyone else is free.

Practitioner: That's a good plan. Is there any kind of reminder you could tell yourself to help you when you're writing the text?

Client: Yeah, maybe some of the positive stuff we talked about, like remembering the good things friends have said about me in the past, so I feel more confident and not so worried about them not replying.

Practitioner: Would it help to write one of those now in a note on your phone?

Client: Okay.

Last, we need to ensure we follow up and ask how home practice tasks have gone. Sometimes sending a reminder summary straight after the session can be helpful. EMHP Nicola Dawson reckons that this helps imbue them with a sense of responsibility. 'It's a bit like passing over the ball,' she says.

And if nothing's been done between sessions – what do we do next?

'I improvise and try to work some into the session!' says Suzanne. 'For example, if we'd agreed they'd do a thought diary and they haven't completed it, I'll ask for some of their most difficult thoughts over the last week. They always manage to give me some that I can jot down to use later in the session.'

Nicola thinks reminding a client of the value of home practice is essential. She says, 'If a client comes back and hasn't done the home practice, I'll tell them I'm glad they've come back and ask "What got in the way?" I remind them that the work is about doing things differently rather than just talking – that's what the research tells us is most effective.'

'I might remind them of their goals, and say, "Okay, let's go back a step. What did you want help with originally?" I might also say, "You need to tell me if it helps or not but first we have to give it a go." It's important to remind them that we need to experiment with change to see if it works.'

WHEN YOU TRY YOUR BEST BUT YOU DON'T SUCCEED

Surprise, surprise – sometimes things get worse. Our intervention is just one tiny piece of the puzzle in a young person's life. And if our client tells us about an unexpected bereavement or some other major event, well it would be weird not to wonder about putting things on hold.

However, if your client's outcome measure scores are resembling the trajectory of a dive-bomber and there's no obvious reason for things getting worse, talk to your supervisor! As Duncan Law says, there's a really unhelpful myth in mental health that we can help everyone get better. We can't. And we shouldn't feel like we're ultimately responsible for every client improving. That would be really unhealthy.

But when things aren't going well there could be a number of factors that need exploring. Perhaps the goal is unrealistic or your expectations for week-by-week progress are too high? Maybe there are ways you could tweak the style of sessions to suit the learning style of your client better – perhaps offering a more visual approach. Maybe there are some issues related to diversity and difference that you haven't considered?

There may also be factors affecting our ability to deliver good work and it's important to be honest with ourselves. As Bennett-Levy and Thwaites (2007) found, life and work stress can sometimes mean practitioners struggle to be empathic. Maybe you're feeling tired or burnt out? Alternatively, perhaps you're not feeling confident enough and could benefit from some further training in a particular intervention – or maybe over-confidence is blinding you!

It could be that our client's not yet ready for change – particularly if it's not their idea to come to sessions in the first place. As EMHP Caroline Carter says, 'If the difficulties have been around a long time, they're not likely going to just change straight away.'

There might be other factors that are getting in the way. Considerations around neurodiversity might need further exploration or even assessment. And if low mood has taken a real plunge, or the anxiety has escalated, or you're spotting signs of OCD, you might consider discussing the value of referring the client to a more specialist CAMHS service (see Chapters 12 and 21).

If things aren't going well, consider asking your client's views around booking in a meeting with the client's parents, key school staff and any other agencies that might be involved. As Suzanne Everill suggests, it's an opportunity to discuss the low intensity treatment, what helped and what to do next.

Suzanne says, 'EMHPs don't need to feel like they have to come up with all of the answers at this point. The school will have their own protocols for putting further support in place. The child's parents often request further help when treatment doesn't seem to improve things and are grateful to have meetings arranged with the school for further advice.'

Basically – if you get stuck, get thinking with your supervisor and open things up. And ultimately if things haven't gone well or it feels like nothing has changed, you may still have planted a seed that will take root after your sessions have ended. As clinical psychologist Sally McGuire puts it, 'You may also have given them a positive experience of CBT that will mean they're more likely to ask for similar help in the future.'

TAKE-AWAYS

▶ It can be frustrating when progress isn't a nice upward curve, but sticking with the difficulty, using open questions and using a motivational interviewing grid will help uncover any potential blocks.

▶ Clients have to appreciate the value of between-session tasks, feel they 'own' the idea and have sufficient motivation to give them a go. Instead of calling it homework, consider 'action steps', 'experiments' or 'positive steps'. And think ahead with the client around any likely issues completing them.

▶ If a client's not making progress or is getting worse, discuss it in supervision and openly wonder about what might be up and try to problem solve it together.

CHAPTER 24

Working Within Schools

A quick warning: anyone walking through the front door of a school wearing an ID badge that says 'mental health practitioner' is going to get mobbed! There's just so much need at the time of writing – and it's unlikely to change. Having said that, you just can't beat being embedded in a good, functioning school that really values the wellbeing of its pupils – it's a fantastic experience. This chapter looks at some of the challenges and potential solutions when working in schools – focusing mainly on secondary schools.

THIS CHAPTER COVERS:

- The importance of whole school approaches
- How to work effectively in school environments
- Working with school avoidance and school exclusions
- How school staff consultations and triage meetings can help with a whole school approach
- Tips on running groups and workshops for young people and parents alike
- How to work with complex bereavements in school communities

WHOLE SCHOOL APPROACHES

For some reason I have Freddie Mercury singing 'Under Pressure' as an earworm whenever I think about the years I spent working in schools. I think it's important to be honest and reflect on the fact that school can be highly stressful for young people and staff alike. Eighty per cent of teenagers say that academic pressure affects their mental health (Cowburn and Blow, 2017) and soberingly, five students in every class of Year 11 students will have a mental health problem (NHS, 2017). Researchers have concluded that 'the stress of exams and the general school experience all contribute towards young people's deteriorating mental health' (McPartlan, 2021, citing the research of Cortina and Lineham, 2021).

One last statistic before we move on – only 50 per cent of students say they'd feel comfortable telling their teachers about mental health issues (Anna Freud Centre, 2021).

So, there's clearly lots of work to be done! And it's not all down to EMHPs and CWPs. Improving a whole school's wellbeing will need amazing leadership and lots of enthusiasm from the headteacher and school staff. There's a whole continuum of ways we can effect change within schools – from posters and social media campaigns through to assemblies, workshops, training, groups and one-to-one work (Nash and Schlosser, 2016 – see Figure 24.1).

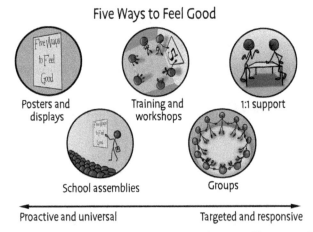

Figure 24.1: There's a variety of ways we can boost wellbeing in schools on a continuum from proactive, universal approaches through to targets and responsive interventions (Nash and Schlosser, 2016)

Obviously – MHSTs are perfectly placed to get stuck in with whole school approaches. But, and it's a big but, with limited resources, practitioners can quickly feel overwhelmed by the scale and breadth of whole school work. It's up to service managers to help bracket the work. If practitioners are running around trying to satisfy the whim of every school request they'll quickly burn out. It's stressful enough trying to plan a group, organise a psychoeducation talk at an assembly and plan your next three one-to-one sessions (perhaps on your own without the support of a colleague) without having to try to prioritise between them. Well – I found my years in an MHST pilot project pretty stressful anyhow! Here are some tips on how to succeed in this demanding environment.

Tip 1: be creative, but stick to the evidence base

My first tip is to stay true to evidence-based practice. It's so tempting to get involved in all kinds of things, but come back to what you know best. There are creative ways of bringing EBP to bear in schools. A recent project in 15 Canadian schools involved a Harry Potter-based mental health literacy curriculum being used to teach CBT skills to 11- to 14-year-olds (Goldstein *et al.*, 2021). The three-month programme reduced depression and anxiety across the year groups, and it also involved wizards. What's not to like?

Lots of evidence-based practice can be really helpful with school-related issues. Some examples include:

- psychoeducation workshops on exam-related anxiety for Year 10 students

- transitions groups for vulnerable Year 6 pupils

- workshops for parents of younger children on parent-led CBT for anxiety

- whole-school assemblies on the 'five ways to wellbeing' model

- 'brain buddies' emotional regulation groups for primary-school children.

Tip 2: get other services involved

How about hooking up with other organisations to enhance whole school approaches? In Brighton, the schools wellbeing service got the council's public health team to set up rock-climbing, skateboard, mountain-biking and wellbeing walk projects in different secondary schools. School wellbeing practitioners weaved some CBT psychoeducation into the sessions. By helping students do some mood monitoring and integrate values-based activities into their weeks, they helped them cope better with exam stress and low mood. You could also link in with local LGBTQ+ charities, faith groups, environmental groups and so on...

Tip 3: involve the young people!

Young people and researchers agree that we need to listen to the views of young people a lot more when thinking about what to offer them. Some schools have a 'wellbeing committee' formed of pupils who can feed back to staff what matters, what works and how to make services more accessible. Young people also need to know that adults are confident, comfortable and non-judgemental about difficult subjects, and adults need to be open and welcoming of mental health conversations.

Tip 4: skill up the staff

Not all staff are comfortable talking about mental health, of course. There's lots of excellent training out there. MindEd[1] has developed e-learning packages to help staff feel more confident in working with mental health issues, and the Anna Freud Centre hosts lots of resources on its website.[2]

While mental health leads should be the ones spearheading efforts to improve the wellbeing and skills of staff, MHST practitioners can really help, too. As Mina Fazel (2021) says, there are many subtle ways teachers can help vulnerable students with their wellbeing – whether by setting up small groups around them or by dedicating time in form time to talk about mental health issues. By offering consultations to staff we can help them with this.

---

1   minded.org.uk
2   mentallyhealthyschools.org.uk

Self-harm is a particularly tricky subject for lots of people. The good news is that we know training really helps. Lots of interventions have been developed to support teachers to feel more confident in these conversations, and a systematic review showed positive impacts across eight different studies (Pierret *et al.*, 2021).

Jaki Watkins is a senior practitioner with ten years' experience in schools. 'Staff feel really stretched,' she says, 'and they need us to support them with resources, and also learning how to maintain boundaries.' This is where school staff consultations can be useful – more on this later.

Tip 5: remember, there's only so much you can do

There is a limit to what you can achieve – it is up to schools, the local authorities and ultimately the government to set the right tone and put child wellbeing at the heart of their priorities. Taking on too much eventually affects our own wellbeing (see Chapter 5!). The best practical advice I've ever heard is to try to deliberately walk slowly through the corridors. And definitely take your breaks outside of the school!

WORKING WITH EMOTIONALLY BASED SCHOOL AVOIDANCE

School avoidance is really tricky for young people, parents and school staff alike. Everyone is under pressure to help a young person get back into school – and some of this comes from the very real threat of penalties being imposed. As such, a 'blame game' can get established, where school staff might blame parents for not being able to get their child in, while a parent might blame their child for not wanting to go – or blame the school for not providing adequate support. Young people can quickly feel like there's something wrong with them for not being able to get into school, while parents can feel guilty around trying to push them. None of it is easy, and we need to be mindful of these dynamics if we do get involved.

As wellbeing practitioners, we need to remember that the young person is our client, and not the school attendance officer. Don't feel persuaded into simply working on behalf of the school to get students back in. So, if you're working with a teenager with social anxiety with a 'poor attendance record', then pay close attention to what really matters to them. When thinking about goals, you might discover their number one priority is to reconnect with their friends and not to get back into school. Go with that. Maybe if things go well, a by-product of our efforts will be that they're back in school – but the goal that matters the most to the young person should matter the most to us, too.

Here's some questions to ponder if you're working with someone who's avoiding school.

- Can you help formulate the push and pull factors? For example, some children are really worried about a parent's mental or physical health. This might not be very obvious, but it might be the reason they want to stay home. Motivational interviewing can be really helpful to understand the young person's voice, what they miss about school and what they want for the future.

- Relationships can sometimes sour between parents and school staff, and it's easy to be positioned in an unhelpful way. How can you stay focused on what the young person wants?

- When a young person has some motivation to return, can you build a back-up team involving school and parents and help them develop a step-by-step approach? Graded exposure can be really helpful (Heyne *et al.*, 2002).

- Have you considered neurodiversity? NICE guidance states that it's quite common for autism to be diagnosed late – particularly in girls. Set your ASC antennae to high sensitivity when thinking about Year 7 and Year 8 pupils who are struggling.

WORKING WITH EXCLUSIONS

Imagine the situation: you've been working with Max, a 15-year-old boy who's struggling with depression. Just before your next session, a teacher pops his head round the door and says, 'Sorry, Max isn't going to make it. He's been permanently excluded after punching a teacher.'

Max lost his older brother to suicide two years ago. Both his parents are unemployed, and his Mum has severe anxiety. You're left fuming. You don't think the school appreciates that his irritability is a symptom of depression, but the teacher says he crossed a line – decision made.

Exclusions can place us in tricky positions, and we know that children with special educational needs – some of our most vulnerable students – are far more likely to be permanently excluded. Here are some ideas on things to consider when working with a young person who's been excluded.

First, how do you feel? School exclusions can trigger strong emotions. Acknowledge your own reactions, discuss the situation in supervision and agree next steps with a cool head.

Second, consider if it's appropriate to try to keep sessions going, perhaps in the community or online. If you can see them again, then review what ongoing support they've got in place – perhaps digging out their back-up team diagram again. They're likely to feel seriously uprooted.

Third, find out if a plan is in place for them to be moved to another local school in what is known as a 'managed move'. You might be able to help your client by having a conversation with their new school about how mental health issues might affect their behaviour (if they agree to you doing so).

Fourth, bear in mind that following a managed move, a young person might develop an idea about themselves as someone who's beyond help. They may not want to accept help from a professional who wears a lanyard and looks a bit like the school staff who excluded them. If you're working with a new client who's been through this kind of experience, discuss the dynamics and what might be helpful with your supervisor.

TIPS FOR RUNNING GROUPS AND WORKSHOPS

Workshops and groups can really boost the number of people our services can reach. Here's some ideas on what can help in practice.

Write up a menu

Don't keep re-inventing the wheel and coming out with endless new PowerPoint presentations! After consulting with young people, school staff and parents your service can hunker down and come up with a limited menu of workshops and groups that practitioners feel confident enough to deliver. You can then email it around and only take orders from schools from the menu! This will really help keep things focused.

Include school staff in planning

Every school is different, and you might not know the intricate details of its PSHE curriculum or what happens during world mental health day or Black history month. Before any new group or workshop, meet up with a school rep and show them your content so they can suggest tweaks. A planning meeting means you'll get to learn about the audience and adapt your group or workshop accordingly. For example, if you're offering a Year 6 transitions workshop for autistic pupils then you'll need to understand the school's existing transition plans and include school visit dates and other details like maps, timetables and even pictures of the secondary school in your presentation.

At the meeting, you'll also want to suss out how teachers will be involved. Agree in advance how you and teachers will work together to manage any challenging behaviour. Teachers are busy and will naturally take advantage of any opportunity to crack on with a bit of marking or lesson preparation!

Parent workshops and groups

Parent workshops and groups give a much-needed space for parents to talk to each other and help each other with similar issues. CBT therapist Zoe Goode reckons creating the space to talk is the most valued aspect of a workshop or group and this is so often reflected in feedback.

'Sometimes it's helpful for parents to stay in touch with each other after a workshop, and you might suggest those that want to form a social media group to keep the support going,' Zoe suggests.

The Anna Freud Centre took this idea one step further and set up 'multi-family groups' in many London primary schools, bringing together families for after-school clubs. Often the network of support continues long after the programmes end, with parents signing up to become facilitators. The project recreates a kind of 'village spirit' where all the parents work together to help raise children.

After running a parent workshop, you might end up with a queue of parents asking you for individual help with their child. Naturally, you might want to help everyone, but try to stick to your boundaries and go through the three steps you've already practised:

1. Acknowledge the difficulty.

2. Explain your role.

3. Signpost the parent or carer on to where they can get further help.

A case study: exam stress workshops

Brighton's schools wellbeing service ran exam stress workshops for Year 10 students in several secondary schools. The single-session workshops included psychoeducation and problem solving. After exploring their common experiences, students were facilitated to discover some common 'vicious circles' of exam anxiety (see Figure 24.2).

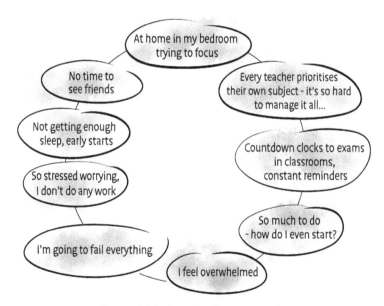

Figure 24.2: A student's vicious cycle

This helped normalise the experience: 'I didn't realise everyone else felt so guilty and stressed,' said one student. Students were then encouraged to think up more healthy revision habits, such as revising in shorter bursts, planning relaxation activities and developing coping skills.

Practitioners fed back student comments to headteachers. In some schools, this led to the removal of 'countdown-to-exam' clocks and teachers changing how they talked about assessments. These were direct improvements in the schools' environments – and hopefully will lead to happier Year 10s in the future.

Advanced skills: school staff consultations

School staff are at the sharp edge of emotional crises and the split between home and school life – particularly in secondary school – can mean that teachers and pastoral staff feel both very responsible and very worried about their students. Offering staff the opportunity to have a consultation with you is one way of easing their load.

Consultations can offer a sense containment (Bion, 1962). As one teacher put it in their feedback, 'I went into the consultation feeling quite anxious, but the session helped me process the feeling and detach a little bit from it – it was good to have a moment to think.'

A consultation can also be a valuable opportunity for reflection – and how rare are those moments in the frantic school day. The same teacher wrote, 'It was good to have new ideas on what to do next, and also to appreciate there's a limit to how much I can do.'

You don't have to be an 'expert'. Simple things can be really helpful. 'I sometimes ask the staff member to draw out their "back-up team" so they can go away and keep looking after themselves,' suggests one EMHP.

Lots of us have that tendency to 'want to get it right' and school staff are no different. Jaki Watkins thinks there's huge therapeutic value in helping staff see what they're already doing well.

'The positives often don't get recognised or remembered as staff rush from one crisis to another,' she says.

You have lots of valuable knowledge to impart, too. As one CWP says, 'Sometimes just sharing some simple psychoeducational concepts on anxiety and depression can be more helpful than you realise.'

Given the pace of schools, it's important to structure a consultation in a professional way – never agree to run one ad hoc in a school corridor. Book a time in, make sure you won't be disturbed, and when you run it, set an agenda and a goal. A consultation template (Table 24.1) will help you structure the conversation and gives you a written record note to share with the consultee and file, too.

✱ Table 24.1: A staff consultation record template

STAFF CONSULTATION FORM	
EMHP:	DATE / TIME:
SCHOOL:	
SCHOOL STAFF NAME:	CONTACT DETAILS:
PUPIL INITIALS:	YEAR GROUP:

Clarification of your role, signposting, and safeguarding

(*E.g. I'm an EMHP working for Carlisle MHST. I'll take notes and I need to keep a record of our chat, and I'd also liase with safeguarding if I have any concerns for anyone's safety of course.*)

'How will we know this conversation has been useful? What do you want to get out of it?'

(*It can be problem solving, ideas for signposting or it could be a chance to reflect – but we need to be clear.*)

'In brief, what is the problem or issue?'
(*Keep the 5WFIDO model in mind to make it specific.*)

Discussion points:

Action points and next steps:

'How useful has this chat been in terms of what you wanted out of it at the start?'

0————————————————————————————————————10

'What's been useful?'

▨ **TRY IT OUT: school staff consultation role play**

Get a colleague to role play a recent case from the point of view of a member of the school staff – either a teacher or pastoral support worker – while as the EMHP you structure and record the consultation using the template. After the exercise, reflect on your experience by answering the following:

- How did you find the experience?

- How did you handle client confidentiality?

- How easy was it to set an agenda and keep to agreed times?

- Did you have any safeguarding concerns? If so, what would you do about them?

- What onward steps and action points did you agree for yourself and the staff member?

- What was it like asking for feedback?

Advanced skills: school triage meetings

In some secondary schools, school staff and mental health professionals meet each week to discuss students of concern. It's likely to be a fast-paced affair rattling through a discussion of 30 or more young people, and it needs to be well chaired with agendas sent out in advance and action points agreed and followed up on.

These triage meetings help in a number of ways:

1. It's a dedicated slot to decide best next steps.

2. It contains staff anxieties and can reduce emails and corridor conversations.

3. It's a collaborative meeting, drawing on a range of different points of view, and reducing the sense of burden individuals can feel for student outcomes.

4. Shared perspectives help increase everyone's individual understandings.

5. Professionals can be kept up to date with waiting lists and current interventions.

6. It's good safeguarding practice to ensure no young person slips through the net.

7. It's a great learning space for staff to be kept up to date with changes in local service offers and referral criteria, and understand signposting ideas for staff to offer to young people, parents and carers.

A referral decision-making tree or flow chart can help clear up any uncertainty around referral pathways. It's easy to forget who does what in wellbeing services – particularly when there are such frequent changes in commissioning, service names and so on.

Advanced skills: ideas around therapeutic support following complex bereavement in school communities

Tragically, sometimes a pupil dies unexpectedly, or a death is not easily explainable, which can lead to complex traumatic bereavement within a school community. Embedded school-based practitioners may be asked to help in the response, so it's important to think ahead about what steps your service would take, should the worst happen.

David Trickey is a clinical psychologist and a trauma specialist – he's frequently asked to get involved by schools after big crises and has provided expert advice after tragic incidents such as the Grenfell Tower disaster. David's first piece of advice is that we should recognise that staff embedded in school have a particularly important role.

'When something terrible has happened, probably the last thing that the kids want is for a stranger to come along and try to fix things, but if there is someone that already knows the schools and is a familiar face around the corridors and may have seen some of the kids directly, then they are much better placed to be helpful,' says David. Friendly faces matter.

Second, it's important that clear guidelines are in place, outlining the responsibilities of the various agencies that support schools. An MHST is just one piece of the puzzle. And while an embedded MHST practitioner is well placed to offer support, actually we need to be really careful that they are not overwhelmed as the nature of their role can increase exposure to demands and stress at these times. As David says, it's important to remember that all school staff can play a big part just by being known and trusted.

Third, if the school does request help, it is important to follow protocols and keep boundaries. Aspects of complex bereavement can take us beyond an MHST's early intervention remit. Jaki Watkins, who has offered support in several traumatic bereavement incidents, recommends that any senior practitioners who are asked to be involved should have some level of bereavement training and understand how adult grief processes can differ from those of young people. Additionally, there will be increased concern around the already-vulnerable students and there might be requests for urgent risk assessments, but Specialist CAMHS services may be better placed to offer these.

If practitioners do offer support within the school, the MHST should ensure sufficient support is provided, including daily check-ins by supervisors to help practitioners process and manage the impact of the trauma on themselves. Practitioners could also consider being physically in school for shorter bursts of time, leaving for frequent breaks to decompress.

It can be easy for practitioners to feel swamped: staff, parents and students alike can struggle. As David points out, 'Bereavement is something that very many staff members may have experienced, so the possibility of their own personal experience of loss being triggered is higher.' Good triaging and signposting really helps. MHSTs could also suggest information for the school to distribute to parents and carers to help them care for their children at home.

Support groups

An MHST might be asked to provide support groups for young people most affected by loss. When thinking about how this might best be done, it is useful to follow the principles set out by a team of expert authors who reviewed the evidence and came up with the following evidence-informed principles (Hobfoll et al., 2007). They recommend applying these five key factors in any therapeutic support:

1. Promote a sense of safety.

2. Promote calming.

3. Promote a sense of self- and collective efficacy.

4. Promote connectedness.

5. Promote help.

By allowing and at times encouraging young people to talk about what they've experienced and how they feel about it, we can help a group foster a sense of connectedness and help individuals support each other, sharing tips around what is helping them through possibly the most difficult experience of their lives. According to David, it's okay to use humour and playfulness when appropriate, even during really heavy sessions. Lighter moments can make it easier for young people to talk through their reactions, thereby helping reduce the impact of any 'stuck' traumatic memories. Allow sufficient space too: it can take several weeks for young people to become familiar with the idea of talking about their experiences.

While they do need some understanding of bereavement and its impact, practitioners don't need to become trauma-focused CBT experts. Many of our existing low intensity skills will help in their own right. Assisting young people to learn and practise coping skills and relaxation activities will help them self-regulate, and problem-solving skills will mean they'll have a better idea of what to do if they're not coping. Meanwhile, help young people enhance their own social support networks, using 'back-up team' social circles exercises, which have good evidence for effectiveness in reducing the prevalence of PTSD. According to Trickey, most children and young people don't develop PTSD after traumatic bereavements because they find a way to process what's happened by talking about it. Conversely, if social support is lacking, the likelihood of developing PTSD increases (Trickey *et al.*, 2012).

TAKE-AWAYS

► As a team, it's important to think about how you will deliver a mix of 'whole school approach' interventions and individual interventions.

► We need to stick to delivering evidence-based interventions but can be creative in how this is done.

► Exam stress groups are a good example of a mental health intervention tailored for a particular need.

► School avoidance and school exclusions need practitioners to think outside the box, but not be pulled into unhelpful dynamics.

► School staff consultations and referral triage meetings can help staff feel supported while keeping a focus on the children's wellbeing.

► A complex or traumatic bereavement requires thought-through responses, and the evidence base points towards the usefulness of groups focusing on social support for traumatically bereaved young people.

Afterword

Thanks for reading this book. I wanted to end by letting you know I think you're amazing for getting involved in mental health work. You are going to change young people's and families' lives. That's pretty cool. Along the way, though, there are going to be some rough moments, so I wanted to share some final thoughts to wrap things up as we say farewell.

MENTAL HEALTH WORK IS TOUGH

I feel bad that the last chapter ended with some fairly heavy stuff, but that is part of the reality of mental health work. So much of the darkness, difficulty and distress we come across in our work is shrouded by words like 'presentation', 'risk', 'safety plan', 'intent' and 'superficial'. These words are as meaningless as they are sanitised – it's as if they've been chosen because they lack any emotional impact. Mental health work can be really tough, and I think it's important to remember and respect this, always – there's nothing wrong with you for feeling emotional, wrung out or even desperate after a difficult session. You're simply a human being, and you need to go talk to someone.

DO A LOT OF A LITTLE, RATHER THAN A LITTLE OF A LOT

Academics can bang on all they like about how whole school approaches can reduce the need for one-to-one interventions, but unless they're at the frontline they'll never understand the real impact of systemic under-funding and what that does to schools and communities.

We cannot possibly do everything that's asked of us. Go back to Chapters 3 and 4 and get even more practice at politely saying 'no'. Try to get good at just a few things – and feel good doing them.

LOOK AFTER YOURSELF, AND YOUR COLLEAGUES

If you don't feel supported and cherished where you work, move on. You cannot battle a toxic culture while trying to help young minds work better; it's just too much. There are plenty of supportive, nurturing teams led by passionate, inspiring practitioners, and you will find your place in one.

'THE FACTS ARE FRIENDLY'

That's a quote from Carl Rogers – the father of person-centred counselling. He advised us to follow the science. I've no doubt that if he was a young teaching assistant in the UK right now, he'd be applying to be a CWP or EMHP. Sooner or later someone's going to persuade you to try out the latest brain-spotting yoga therapy which is apparently just fantastic. Don't let your head be turned: have faith in evidence-based practice and give it your best shot.

BE AS KIND AS YOU CAN

We don't always remember what people teach us, but we do remember how people treat us. It's not always easy to be kind, but midway through a session, if you start feeling tense and bothered because you're not getting through the manual, well, drop the manual like a hot stone and focus on just being with the person you're with, listening to them and validating them. Then pick the manual up again when you're both ready for it.

KEEP LEARNING

The best therapists are always learning. Try to be encouraging to yourself as you try out new skills and always have new competencies in mind that you want to develop. It's okay to re-read a book or watch a ten-minute clip of an intervention online just before trying it out in a session (particularly if your brain's like a sieve, like mine).

PETS ARE GOOD CO-THERAPISTS

If your pet cat, dog or iguana walks across your keyboard during an online session, don't fret. It's probably good for the working alliance. Again, this hasn't been properly researched, so take this with a pinch of salt – but pet appearances tend to work out okay. As long as you're not on screen while your labrador's giving birth to nine puppies, I guess.

KEEP SHARING

Despite it being very early days, there's such an incredible wealth of experience among low intensity practitioners already. Let's keep sharing it and helping each other develop in our common mission to improve the lives of children and young people.

AND LAST OF ALL...

'Be yourself. Everyone else is taken.' – Oscar Wilde

Acronym and Jargon Buster

ADHD Attention deficit hyperactivity disorder.

AN Anorexia nervosa, an eating disorder categorised by low weight, restricted eating and a fear of gaining weight.

AOT An assertive outreach team is for young people with severe mental health needs that are seriously affecting their ability to manage their daily lives.

ASC Autistic spectrum condition (previously or sometimes known as ASD).

Attachment theory Looks at how our early life experiences shape our way of relating to others.

Attention-seeking behaviour An outdated term used to describe a young person's actions that could be better described as 'care-seeking' or 'connection-seeking'.

Behavioural activation Doing more of what matters to improve low mood.

Blueprinting The work of reviewing what's helped in therapy and what's important to remember going forward.

Bulimia Bulimia Nervosa is an eating disorder involving binge-eating and purging.

C-PTSD Complex post-traumatic stress disorder, usually resulting from multiple significant traumas.

CAMHS Child and Adolescent Mental Health Services.

Capacity The ability to make your own choices and decisions.

CBT Cognitive behavioural therapy.

CIC Children in care.

Co-morbidity Having two conditions at once, e.g. anxiety and depression. Very common!

CORC Child Outcomes Research Consortium.

CORS Child Outcome Rating Scales.

Creative Therapies Includes art, drama and music therapies – often drawing on a range of psychotherapy models with parallels to integrative psychotherapy.

CWP Children's wellbeing practitioner.

CYP-IAPT You do the maths!

CYP Children and young people, or child/young person.

DDP Dyadic developmental psychotherapy, the brainchild of Dan Hughes – great for helping repair attachment difficulties.

Depression Low mood and depression are often used interchangeably.

Early intervention Acting early to prevent things getting worse.

EBP Evidence-based practice. Using the best available evidence to inform practice.

EBPU Evidence-based practice unit.

ED Eating disorder.

EHCP An 'education, health and care plan'.

EMHP Education mental health practitioner.

FE Further education (for 16-year-olds+).

Functional Analysis Looking at what 'function' a behaviour or dynamic might serve. For example, self-harm sometimes helps distract a YP from emotional pain or might be a care-seeking behaviour.

GAD Generalised anxiety disorder.

Gillick-competent A term used when thinking about whether a child is mature enough to make decisions that affect them or sign up for treatment without their parents/carers knowing or consenting.

Graded exposure therapy Facing fears, step by step, to overcome the effects of anxiety.

HASQ Helpful aspects of supervision questionnaire. Four questions asked at the end of a supervision session to check out how it's gone.

IA An initial assessment.

IAPT Improving Access to Psychological Therapies – a programme to increase the amount of evidence-based talking therapies available to people.

In-patient care Psychiatric wards are within Tier 4 services, and provide specialist treatment for eating disorders, for example.

IPT Interpersonal psychotherapy (specifically used for depression).

KCL Kings College London.

LA Local authority – this generally means the local council, which usually employs social services.

LAC A looked after child or looked after children (children in care).

LADO Local authority designated safeguarding officer.

LD Learning difficulty or disability.

Lead professional Also known as a lead practitioner – the central person in providing and coordinating someone's care.

MASH A multi-agency safeguarding hub. A single point of contact in a local area for safeguarding concerns, often with a helpful phone line for you to discuss concerns.

Mentalisation The ability to perceive and to communicate one's own mental states and those of others – the ability to be 'mindful of minds'.

MH Mental health.

MHST Mental health support team.

Neurodiversity A term that recognises the variations in how all our brains and minds work.

Neuroscience The scientific study of the brain, its structure and its functioning.

NHS The UK's National Health Service.

NICE The 'National Institute for Clinical Excellence' provides guidance to the NHS on what treatments to provide.

OCD Obsessive compulsive disorder.

OT An occupational therapist.

Primary care Services like GPs, school nurses and MHSTs that provide first-step interventions.

PRU Pupil referral unit.

Psychodynamic/psychoanalytic Involves thinking about the unconscious and the dynamics between the therapist and client (transference, projection, projective identification, etc.).

PTSD Post-traumatic stress disorder.

Quantitative research Research that collects information that can be measured (e.g. it involves numbers, as opposed to qualitative, which doesn't).

RCT A randomised control trial. The gold standard in intervention evaluation as used in vaccine development, etc. 'Double blind' means the participants in both groups are in the dark as to what they're getting.

RCADS Revised children's anxiety and depression scale.

RMN Registered mental health nurse.

ROMS Routine outcome measures.

SH Self-harm.

SI Suicidal ideation, or 'thinking about wanting to die'. *Or* 'serious incident', as in serious incident reviews.

SAD Social anxiety disorder. SAD can also refer to seasonal affective disorder.

Safeguarding The process of ensuring CYPs at risk are kept safe. Everyone's responsibility!

SAGE A scale for rating a supervisor's competence in delivering supervision.

Secondary care Also known as Tier 2 and Tier 3 services, including Specialist CAMHS and outpatient departments.

SEMH Social, emotional and mental health difficulties.

SEN Special educational need.

SENCO A teacher in a school responsible for special educational needs coordination.

SEND Special educational need or disability.

Session zero The first session in a presentation-specific intervention, often following a more generic 'initial assessment'. In some manuals, a session zero is bolted on in front of an eight-session intervention.

Signposting Pointing someone on to another service that might be helpful.

Social prescribing When professionals refer people to support in the community.

SRS Session rating scales.

SS Social services.

SSEN Statement of special education need.

Systemic Therapy Also known as family therapy.

TAC Team around the child.

Theory of mind The ability to understand others have beliefs, desires and intentions that are different from one's own.

Third sector Also known as the voluntary sector. Several charities receive government funding to provide wellbeing services.

Triaging Discussing young people and deciding what interventions to offer whom, often done by a group in a weekly meeting.

UCL University College London.

Unconscious bias How our background and own experiences shape what we assume about someone else.

VIG Video interaction guidance. A NICE-recommended, strengths-based approach for working with attachment difficulties with younger children in care and their parents/carers.

Wellbeing Having good physical and mental health.

Young Minds A leading young people's mental health charity with a very useful website for professionals, children and young people.

References

Anna Freud Centre (2020). *The EMHP Competency Framework*. Retrieved from https://manuals.annafreud.org/emhp/index.html

Anna Freud Centre (2021). *Working towards Mentally Healthy Schools and FE Colleges: The Voice of Students*. Retrieved from https://mentallyhealthyschools.org.uk/resources/working-towards-mentally-healthy-schools-and-fe-colleges-the-voice-of-students

APA, Presidential Task Force on Evidence-Based Practice (2006). Evidence-based practice in psychology. *The American Psychologist 61*, 4, 271–285. https://doi.org/10.1037/0003-066X.61.4.271

Barker, H., Bowyer, L., Payne, S., Williams, S. *et al.* (2021). *Getting to Grips with Anxiety: A Guided Self-Help Workbook*. London: King's College London and Anna Freud Centre.

BBC (2019). Greta Thunberg's father: 'She is happy, but I worry'. Retrieved from www.bbc.co.uk/news/uk-50901789

Beaumont, E. and Welford, M. (2020). *The Kindness Workbook: Creative and Compassionate Ways to Boost Your Wellbeing*. London: Robinson.

Beck, A.T., Rush, A.J., Shaw, B.F. and Emery, G. (1979). *Cognitive Therapy of Depression*. New York: The Guilford Press.

Beck, A., Naz, S., Brooks, M. and Jankowska, M. (2019). *IAPT Black, Asian and Minority Ethnic Service User Positive Practice Guide*. Retrieved from https://babcp.com/Therapists/BAME-Positive-Practice-Guide

Bennett-Levy, J. and Thwaites, R. (2007). Self and Self-Reflection in the Therapeutic Relationship: A Conceptual Map and Practical Strategies for the Training, Supervision and Self-Supervision of Interpersonal Skills. In P. Gilbert and R.L. Leahy (eds), *The Therapeutic Relationship in the Cognitive Behavioral Psychotherapies*. Abingdon, New York: Routledge, Taylor & Francis Group.

Berry, K., Law, H. and Ryan, R. (2021). Therapeutic relationships in child and adolescent mental health services: A Delphi study with young people, carers and practitioners. *International Journal of Mental Health Nursing 30*, 4, 1010–1021. Retrieved from https://onlinelibrary.wiley.com/doi/full/10.1111/inm.12857

Bion, W.R. (1962). *Learning from Experience*. London: Karnac Books.

Brachtel, D. and Richter, E. (1992). Absolute bioavailability of caffeine from a tablet formulation. *Journal of Hepatology 16*, 3, 385. Retrieved from https://pubmed.ncbi.nlm.nih.gov/1487618

Brett, S., Pass, L., Reynolds, S. and Totman, J. (2020). Brief behavioural activation therapy for adolescent depression in schools: Two case examples. *Emotional and Behavioural Difficulties 25*, 3–4, 291–303. doi: 10.1080/13632752.2020.1861853

Brown, L. (2020). Diversity and difference training. Lecture, Anna Freud Centre. 6 November 2020.

Burnett, D. (2019). *Why Your Parents Are Driving You Up the Wall and What to Do About It*. London: Penguin.

Burnham, J. (2012). Developments in Social GRRRAAACCEEESSS: Visible – Invisible and Voiced – Unvoiced. In I.-B. Krause (ed.), *Culture and Reflexivity in Contemporary Systemic Psychotherapy: Mutual Perspectives.* London: Karnac.

Carona, C., Rijo, D., Salvador, C., Castilho, P. and Gilbert, P. (2017). Compassion-focused therapy with children and adolescents. *BJPsych Advances 23,* 4, 240–252. doi: 10.1192/apt.bp.115.015420

Cash, S.J. and Bridge, J.A. (2009). Epidemiology of youth suicide and suicidal behavior. *Current Opinion in Pediatrics 21,* 5, 613–619. https://doi.org/10.1097/MOP.0b013e32833063e1

Chorpita, B.F., Yim, L.M., Moffitt, C.E., Umemoto, L.A. and Francis, S.E. (2000). Assessment of symptoms of DSM-IV anxiety and depression in children: A revised child anxiety and depression scale. *Behaviour Research and Therapy 38,* 835–855.

Compas, B.E., Connor-Smith, J.K., Saltzman, H., Thomsen, A.H. and Wadsworth, M.E. (2001). Coping with stress during childhood and adolescence: Problems, progress, and potential in theory and research. *Psychological Bulletin 127,* 1, 87–127.

Cowburn, A. and Blow, M. (2017). *Wise up: Prioritising Wellbeing in Schools.* Retrieved from www.readkong.com/page/wise-up-prioritising-wellbeing-in-schools-7256446

Craig, T., Garety, P., Waller, H., Jolley, S. *et al.* (2012). *Reaching My Goals One Step at a Time: Therapist Handbook.* London: Centre for Psychological Therapies for Psychosis, Institute of Psychiatry, King's College London.

Cresswell, C. (2021). Brief guided parent-delivered treatment of childhood anxiety: Working collaboratively through parents. Lecture, Anna Freud Centre/Zoom. 23 February 2021.

Cresswell, C. and Willetts, L. (2007). *Overcoming Your Child's Fear and Worries: A Self-Help Guide Using Cognitive Behavioral Techniques.* London: Constable & Robinson.

Cresswell, C. and Willetts, L. (2019). *Helping Your Child with Fears and Worries: A Self-Help Guide for Parents.* London: Little, Brown.

Cresswell, C., Parkinson, M., Thirlwell, K. and Willetts, L. (2017). *Parent-Led CBT for Child Anxiety.* New York: The Guildford Press.

Creswell, C., Waite, P. and Hudson, J. (2020). Practitioner review: Anxiety disorders in children and young people – assessment and treatment. *Journal of Child Psychology and Psychiatry 61,* 628–643. https://doi.org/10.1111/jcpp.13186

Cromar, A. (2020). 'A Harsh wake-up': Here's how white people can broach difficult conversations about race. *Boston.com.* Retrieved from https://www.boston.com/news/local-news/2020/06/16/a-harsh-wake-up-heres-how-white-people-can-broach-difficult-conversations-about-race

De Cou, C.R. and Schumann, M.E. (2017). On the iatrogenic risk of assessing suicidality: A meta-analysis. *Suicide and Life-Threat Behavior 48,* 531–543. https://doi.org/10.1111/sltb.12368

Derisley, J., Heyman, I., Robinson, R. and Turner, C. (2008). *Breaking Free from OCD: A CBT Guide for Young People and Their Families.* London: Jessica Kingsley Publishers.

DfE (2012). *A Profile of Pupil Exclusions in England.* Ref: DFE-RR190. Retrieved from www.gov.uk/government/publications/a-profile-of-pupil-exclusions-in-england

DoE (2016). *Counselling in Schools. A Blueprint for the Future.* Retrieved from https://www.gov.uk/government/publications/counselling-in-schools

DoH/DfE (2017). *Transforming Children and Young People's Mental Health Provision: A Green Paper.* Retrieved from https://assets.publishing.service.gov.uk/government/uploads/system/uploads/attachment_data/file/664855/Transforming_children_and_young_people_s_mental_health_provision.pdf

Doward, J. (2019). Therapy saved a refugee child. *The Observer,* 27 April 2019. Retrieved from www.theguardian.com/society/2019/apr/27/peter-fonagy-refugee-child-psychologist-anna-freud-centre

Eastwood, L., Friedberg, R.D., McLachlan, R. and Lynne, N. (2016). Socratic questions with children: Recommendations and cautionary tales. *Journal of Cognitive Psychotherapy 30,* 2, 105–119.

Eelen, P. and Vervliet, B. (2006). Fear Conditioning and Clinical Implications: What Can We Learn from the Past? In M.G. Craske, D. Hermans and D. Vansteenwegen (eds), *Fear and Learning: From Basic Processes to Clinical Implications.* Washington, DC: American Psychological Association.

Farias, M. and Wikholm, C. (2016). Has the science of mindfulness lost its mind? *BJPsych Bulletin 40*, 6, 329–332. doi: 10.1192/pb.bp.116.053686

Fazel, M. (2021). Literature review of support tools for school staff to respond to CYP self-harm. CAMHS around the Campfire: Lecture/Zoom. 26 April 2021.

Fisk, J., Ellis, J. and Reynolds, S. (2019). A test of the CaR-FA-X mechanisms and depression in adolescents, *Memory 27*, 4, 455–464. doi: 10.1080/09658211.2018.1518457

Fuggle, P., Dunsmuir, S. and Curry, V. (2012). *CBT with Children, Young People & Families*. London: Sage.

Germer, C. (2009). *The Mindful Path to Self-Compassion: Freeing Yourself from Destructive Thoughts and Emotions*. London: The Guilford Press.

Gilbert, P. (2009). *The Compassionate Mind: A New Approach to Life's Challenges*. London: Constable-Robinson.

Goldstein, B.I., Fefergrad, M., Niederkrotenthaler, T. and Sinyor, M. (2021). The Impact of a Harry Potter-Based Cognitive Behavioral Therapy Skills Curriculum on Suicidality and Well-being in Middle Schoolers: A Randomized Controlled Trial. *Journal of Affective Disorders 286*, 134–141. https://doi.org/10.1016/j.jad.2021.02.028

Goodyer, I.M., Reynolds, S., Barrett, B., Byford, S. *et al.* (2017). Cognitive behavioural therapy and short-term psychoanalytical psychotherapy versus a brief psychosocial intervention in adolescents with unipolar major depressive disorder (IMPACT): A multicentre, pragmatic, observer-blind, randomised controlled superiority trial. *The Lancet Psychiatry 4*, 2, 109–119.

Grey, N. [@ndgrey] (2021). I've posted this before but ties in with this webinar so here it is again. Some principles of CBT... [Tweet]. *Twitter*, 17 February. Retrieved from https://twitter.com/nickdgrey/status/1362166889972170756/photo/1

Halldorsson, B., Elliot, L., Chessell, C., Willetts, L. and Creswell, C. (2019). *Helping Your Child with Fears and Worries: A Self-Help Guide for Parents. Treatment Manual for Therapists*. Available under license. London: Robinson.

Heyne, D., King, N.J., Tonge, B.J., Rollings, S. *et al.* (2002). Evaluation of child therapy and caregiver training in the treatment of school refusal. *Journal of the American Academy of Child & Adolescent Psychiatry 41*, 6, 687–695.

Hobfoll, S.E., Watson, P., Bell, C.C., Bryant, R.A. *et al.* (2007). Five essential elements of immediate and mid-term mass trauma intervention: Empirical evidence. *Psychiatry 70*, 4, 283–369. https://doi.org/10.1521/psyc.2007.70.4.283

Horvath, A.O. and Luborsky, L. (1993). The role of the therapeutic alliance in psychotherapy. *Journal of Consulting and Clinical Psychology 61*, 4, 561–573. https://doi.org/10.1037/0022-006X.61.4.561

Hoskins, M.L. (1999). Worlds apart and lives together: Developing cultural attunement. *Child & Youth Care Forum 28*, 2, 73–85. doi: 10.1023/A:1021937105025

Inkelis, S.M., Ancoli-Israel, S., Thomas, J.D. and Bhattacharjee, R. (2021). Elevated risk of depression among adolescents presenting with sleep disorders. *Journal of Clinical Sleep Medicine 17*, 4, 675–683. https://doi.org/10.5664/jcsm.8996

Kennedy, H., Landor, M. and Todd, L. (2011). *Video Interaction Guidance: A Relationship-Based Intervention to Promote Attunement, Empathy and Wellbeing*. London: Jessica Kingsley Publishers.

Kennerley, H. (2007). *Socratic Method*. Oxford: Oxford Cognitive Therapy Centre.

Kennerley, H. (2014). 'Developing and Maintaining a Working Alliance in CBT.' In A. Whittington and N. Grey (eds) *How to Become a More Effective CBT Therapist: Mastering Metacompetence in Clinical Practice*. Chichester: Wiley Blackwell.

Kirby, J.N. (2016). Compassion interventions: The programmes, the evidence, and implications for research and practice. *Psychology & Psychotherapy 90*, 3, 432–455. doi: 10.1111/papt.12104

Klim-Conforti, P., Zaheer, R., Levitt, A.J., Cheung, A. *et al.* (2021). The impact of a Harry Potter-based cognitive-behavioral therapy skills curriculum on suicidality and well-being in middle schoolers: A randomized controlled trial. *Journal of Affective Disorders 28*, 6, 134–141. https://doi.org/10.1016/j.jad.2021.02.028

Kolts, R.L. (2016). *CFT Made Simple: A Clinician's Guide to Practicing Compassion-Focused Therapy*. Oakland, CA: New Harbinger Publications.

Kumar, S., Sherman, L.W. and Strang, H. (2020). Racial disparities in homicide victimisation rates: How to improve transparency by the Office of National Statistics in England and Wales. *Cambridge Journal of Evidence-Based Policing 4* (3–4), 178–186. https://doi.org/10.1007/s41887-020-00055-y

Law, D. (2021). Outcomes and supervision. Lecture, Anna Freud Centre. 27 April 2021.

Law, D. and Jacob, J. (2015). *Goals and Goal Based Outcomes: Some Useful Information* (3rd edn). Retrieved from www.corc.uk.net/media/1219/goalsandgbos-thirdedition.pdf

Law, D. and Wolpert, M. (2014). *Guide to Using Outcomes and Feedback Tools with Children, Young People and Families*. Retrieved from www.corc.uk.net/media/2112/201404guide_to_using_outcomes_measures_and_feedback_tools-updated.pdf

Law, R. (2021). Building a back-up team. CWP lecture, Anna Freud Centre. 9 February 2021.

Lee, D. (2017). An interpretive case study to explore children's, teachers' and parents' experiences and perspectives on the impact of a positive psychology technique called the 'three good things in life' technique. Prof Doc Thesis, University of East London Psychology. https://doi.org/10.15123/PUB.7311

Lister, K. (2020). 'I was diagnosed with ADHD aged 35 – the biggest hurdle was convincing everyone it's real'. *i*, 15 July 2020. https://inews.co.uk/opinion/adhd-diagnosis-adults-symptoms-treatment-dyslexia-498900

Maddox, L., Gutierrez, L., Loades, M., Boyd, A., Thompson, S. and Reynolds, S. (2021). *CBT with Children, Young People and Families: BABCP Good Practice Guide*. Bury: BABCP.

Maiden, Z. (2021). *Behavioural Activation for Young People with Low Mood: Guided Self-Help Manual*. N&S CAMHS Trauma, Anxiety and Depression (TAD) Clinic, South London and Maudsley NHS Trust. Retrieved from https://manuals.annafreud.org/emhp/index.html

McCauley, E., Gudmundsen, G., Schloredt, K., Martell, C. *et al.* (2015). The Adolescent Behavioral Activation Program: Adapting behavioral activation as a treatment for depression in adolescence. *Journal of Clinical Child and Adolescent Psychology 45*, 3, 291–304. https://doi.org/10.1080/15374416.2014.979933

McLachlan, N.H., Eastwood, L. and Friedberg, R.D. (2016). Socratic questions with children: Recommendations and cautionary tales. *Journal of Cognitive Psychotherapy 30*, 2, 105–119.

McPartlan, D. (2021). *Mental Health in Schools: Learning Lessons from the Past*. Retrieved from 10.13056/acamh.15247

Melton, T.H., Croarkin, P.E., Strawn, J.R. and McClintock, S.M. (2016). Comorbid anxiety and depressive symptoms in children and adolescents: A systematic review and analysis. *Journal of Psychiatric Practice 22*, 2, 84–98.

Miller, S.D., Duncan, B.L. and Johnson, L.D. (2000). *The Session Rating Scale 3.0*. Chicago, IL: Authors.

Mir, G., Meer, S., Cottrell, D., McMillan, D., House, A. and Kanter, J.W. (2015). Adapted behavioural activation for the treatment of depression in Muslims. *Journal of Affective Disorders 180*, 190–199. https://doi.org/10.1016/j.jad.2015.03.060

Mobbs, D., Hagan, C.C., Dalgleish, T., Silston, B. and Prévost, C. (2015). The ecology of human fear: Survival optimization and the nervous system. *Frontiers in Neuroscience 9*, 55. https://doi.org/10.3389/fnins.2015.00055

Monk, C.S., McClure, E.B., Nelson, E.E., Zarahn, E. *et al.* (2003). Adolescent immaturity in attention-related brain engagement to emotional facial expressions. *NeuroImage 20*, 1, 420–428. https://doi.org/10.1016/s1053-8119(03)00355-0

Moorey, S. (2010). The six cycles maintenance model: Growing a 'vicious flower' for depression. *Behavioural and Cognitive Psychotherapy 38*, 2, 173.

Murray, L., Creswell, C. and Cooper, P.J. (2009). The development of anxiety disorders in childhood: An integrative review. *Psychological Medicine 39*, 9, 1413–1423. https://doi.org/10.1017/S0033291709005157

Murre, J.M.J. (2015). *Ebbinghaus (1880) Replication*. Retrieved from osf.io/6kfrp

Mynors-Wallis, L. and Lau, M.A. (2010). Problem Solving as a Low Intensity Intervention. In J. Bennett-Levy, D.A. Richards, P. Farrand, H. Christensen *et al.* (eds), *Oxford Guides in Cognitive Behavioural Therapy: Oxford Guide to Low Intensity CBT Interventions*. Oxford: Oxford University Press.

Nash, P.R.G. and Schlosser, A. (2016). Working with Schools in Identifying and Overcoming Emotional Barriers to Learning. In K. Reid (ed.), *Managing and Improving School Attendance and Behaviour: New Approaches and Initiatives*. London: Routledge.

Naz, S. (2021). Where am I really from? *CBT Today 49*, 1, February.

Neff, K.D. and Dahm, K.A. (2015). Self-Compassion: What It Is, What It Does, and How It Relates to Mindfulness. In B.D. Ostafin, M.D. Robinson and B.P. Meier (eds), *Handbook of Mindfulness and Self-Regulation*. New York: Springer.

Neff, K. (2011). *Self-Compassion: The Proven Power of Being Kind to Yourself*. New York: William Morrow.

NHS (2017). *Mental Health of Children and Young People in England*. Retrieved from https://digital.nhs.uk/data-and-information/publications/statistical/mental-health-of-children-and-young-people-in-england/2017/2017#summary

NHS (2020). *Healthy Sleep Tips for Children*. Retrieved from https://www.nhs.uk/live-well/sleep-and-tiredness/healthy-sleep-tips-for-children

NICE (2005). *Obsessive-compulsive disorder and body dysmorphic disorder: Treatment*. Retrieved from https://www.nice.org.uk/guidance/cg31

NICE (2018). *Attention Deficit Hyperactivity Disorder: Diagnosis and Management*. Retrieved from https://www.nice.org.uk/guidance/ng87/chapter/Recommendations#recognition-identification-and-referral

NICE (2019). *Depression in Children and Young People: Identification and Management*. Retrieved from https://www.nice.org.uk/guidance/ng134

O'Connor, R. (2019). *Understanding Suicidal Behaviour*. Retrieved from: www.youtube.com/watch?v=Mhu0Rqgu2Sg

O'Connor, R. (2021). *When It Is Darkest*. London: Penguin.

Odgers, K., Dargue, N., Creswell, C., Jones, M.P. and Hudson, J.L. (2020). The limited effect of mindfulness-based interventions on anxiety in children and adolescents: A meta-analysis. *Clinical Child and Family Psychology Review 23*, 407–426. https://doi.org/10.1007/s10567-020-00319-z

Orchard, F., Pass, L., Chessell, C., Moody, A., Ellis, J. and Reynolds, S. (2019). Adapting brief CBT-I for depressed adolescents: A case illustration of the sleeping better program. *Cognitive and Behavioral Practice 27*, 3, 336–346. https://doi.org/10.1016/j.cbpra.2019.07.010

Orchard, F., Gregory, A.M., Gradisar, M. and Reynolds, S. (2020). Self-reported sleep patterns and quality amongst adolescents: Cross-sectional and prospective associations with anxiety and depression. *The Journal of Child Psychology and Psychiatry 61*, 10, 1126–1137. https://doi.org/10.1111/jcpp.13288

Padesky, C.A. (1993). Socratic questioning: Changing minds or guiding discovery? Invited keynote address presented at the 1993 European Congress of Behaviour and Cognitive Therapies, London. Retrieved from www.padesky.com/clinicalcorner

Padesky, C.A. (2020a). *Supercharge Activity Scheduling (CBT Tip)*. Retrieved from https://m.youtube.com/watch?v=Pzci4D5PHlk&feature=youtu.be

Padesky, C.A. (2020b). *Understanding Anxiety and the the Anxiety Equation (Padesky Clinical Tip Part 1)*. Retrieved from www.youtube.com/watch?v=jw0ivpUQ43U

Pass, L. and Reynolds, S. (2020). *Brief Behavioural Activation for Adolescent Depression*. London: Jessica Kingsley Publishers.

Pass, L., Brisco, G. and Reynolds, S. (2015). Adapting brief behavioural activation (BA) for adolescent depression: A case example. *The Cognitive Behaviour Therapist 8*, E17. https://doi.org/10.1017/S1754470X15000446

Pierret, A.C.S., Anderson, J.K., Ford, T.J. and Burn, A.-M. (2021). Review: Education and training interventions, and support tools for school staff to adequately respond to young people who disclose self-harm – a systematic literature review of effectiveness, feasibility and acceptability. *Child and Adolescent Mental Health*. https://doi.org/10.1111/camh.12436

Place2Be (2021). A third of parents are embarrassed to seek mental health support for their children. Retrieved from www.childrensmentalhealthweek.org.uk/news/a-third-of-parents-are-embarrassed-to-seek-mental-health-support-for-their-children

Riggs, D.W. and Bartholomaeus, C. (2016). Australian mental health professionals' competencies for working with trans clients: A comparative study. *Psychology & Sexuality 7*, 3, 225–238.

Rogers, C.R. (1951). *Client-Centered Therapy: Its Current Practice, Implications, and Theory*. Boston, MA: Houghton Mifflin.

Rosen, M. (2021). *Many Different Kinds of Love*. London: Ebury Press.

Roth, A. and Fonagy, P. (2005). *What Works for Whom: A Critical Review of Psychotherapy Research* (2nd edn). New York: Guilford Publications.

Ryan, R., Berry, K., Law, H. and Hartley, S. (2021). Therapeutic relationships in child and adolescent mental health services: A Delphi study with young people, carers and clinicians. *International Journal of Mental Health Nursing 30*, 4, 1010–1021. https://doi: 10.1111/inm.12857

Sanders, M.R. and Mazzucchelli, T.G. (2018). *The Power of Positive Parenting: Transforming the Lives of Children, Parents and Communities Using the Triple P System*. Oxford: Oxford University Press.

Schmidt, U., Simic, M. and Taylor, L. (2015). *Cutting Down: A CBT Workbook for Treating Young People Who Self-Harm*. Hove: Routledge.

Seligman, M.E., Steen, T.A., Park, N. and Peterson, C. (2005). Positive psychology progress: Empirical validation of interventions. *American Psychologist 60*, 5, 410.

Sherbin, L. and Rashid, R. (2017). Diversity doesn't stick without inclusion. *Harvard Business Review 1*. Retrieved from https://hbr.org/2017/02/diversity-doesnt-stick-without-inclusion

Smith, M.T., Perlis, M.L., Park, A., Smith, M.S. *et al.* (2002). Comparative meta-analysis of pharmacotherapy and behavior therapy for persistent insomnia. *American Journal of Psychiatry 159*, 1, 5–11.

Solmi, M., Radua, J., Olivola, M., Croce, E. *et al.* (2021). Age at onset of mental disorders worldwide: Large-scale meta-analysis of 192 epidemiological studies. *Molecular Psychiatry*. https://doi.org/10.1038/s41380-021-01161-7

Stallard, P. (2005). *A Clinician's Guide to Think Good-Feel Good: Using CBT with Children and Young People*. Chichester: Wiley.

Strauss, P., Lin, A., Winter, S., Waters, Z. *et al.* (2021). Options and realities for trans and gender diverse young people receiving care in Australia's mental health system: Findings from Trans Pathways. *Australian and New Zealand Journal of Psychiatry 55*, 4, 391–399.

Suddendorf, T. and Corballis, M.C. (2007). The evolution of foresight: What is mental time travel, and is it unique to humans? *The Behavioral and Brain Sciences 30*, 3, 299–351. https://doi.org/10.1017/S0140525X07001975

Thirlwall, K., Cooper, P.J., Karalus, J., Voysey, M., Willetts, L. and Creswell, C. (2013). Treatment of child anxiety disorders via guided parent-delivered cognitive-behavioural therapy: Randomised controlled trial. *The British Journal of Psychiatry 203*, 6, 436–444. https://doi.org/10.1192/bjp.bp.113.126698

Trickey, D., Siddaway, A.P., Meiser-Stedman, R., Serpell, L. and Field, A.P. (2012). Meta-analysis of risk factors for PTSD in trauma exposed children. *Clinical Psychology Review 32*, 122–138.

Veale, D. (2008). Behavioural activation for depression. *Advances in Psychiatric Treatment 14*, 29–36. Retrieved from www.veale.co.uk/wp-content/uploads/2010/10/60-BA-for-depression-.pdf

Veale, D. (2021). *Getting a Good Night's Sleep*. Retrieved from www.youtube.com/watch?v=KQzMxFr2xmU

Verduyn, C., Rogers, J. and Wood, A. (2009). *Depression: CBT with Children and Young People*. Hove: Routledge.

Waite, P.L. and Williams, T.I. (2009). *Obsessive Compulsive Disorder: Cognitive Behaviour Therapy with Children and Young People*. Hove: Routledge.

Walker, M. (2018). *Why We Sleep*. London: Penguin Books.

White, M. and Epston, D. (1990). *Narrative Means to Therapeutic Ends*. New York: W.W. Norton.

Whittington, A. and Grey, N. (2014). Mastering Metacompetence: The Science and Art of Cognitive Behavioural Therapy. In A. Whittington and N. Grey (eds), *How to Become a More Effective CBT Therapist: Mastering Metacompetence in Clinical Practice*. Chichester: Wiley Blackwell.

Winnicott, D.W. (1963). Dependence in infant care, in child care, and in the psycho-analytic setting. *The International Journal of Psychoanalysis 44*, 3, 339–344.

Winsler, A., Deutsch, A., Vorona, R.D., Payne, P.A. and Szklo-Coxe, M. (2015). Sleepless in Fairfax: The difference one more hour of sleep can make for teen hopelessness, suicidal ideation, and substance use. *Journal of Youth and Adolescence 44*, 2, 362–378. https://doi.org/10.1007/s10964-014-0170-3

Yalom, I.D. (1989). *Love's Executioner, and Other Tales of Psychotherapy*. New York: HarperPerennial.

Further Reading and Resources

GENERAL GUIDANCE

It's definitely worth spending time reading up on current NICE guidance for different mental health difficulties: www.nice.org.uk
There are lots of amazing resources, videos and guidance specifically for CWPs and EMHPs at: https://manuals.annafreud.org

Try to persuade your service to sign up to Psychology Tools®: www.psychologytools.com

The Get Self Help website is also good: www.getselfhelp.co.uk

MANUALS

Brief Behavioural Activation for Adolescent Depression (2020) by Laura Pass and Shirley Reynolds is your one-stop shop for working with low mood.

If you're working with parents to help younger children with anxiety, you'll need to equip them with *Helping Your Child with Fears and Worries* (2019) by Cathy Creswell and Lucy Willetts. You'll also need either *Parent-led CBT for Child Anxiety* (Cresswell *et al.*, 2017) or the condensed therapist manual, available through some universities.

For challenging behaviour, you'll need a guide such as *The Incredible Years* by Carolyn Webster-Stratton (2006), or *The Power of Positive Parenting: Transforming the Lives of Children, Parents and Communities Using the Triple P System* (Sanders and Mazzuchelli, 2018).

'Open source' EMHP and CWP manuals for low mood and anxiety and materials are available here (check terms and conditions first): https://manuals.annafreud.org. These include *Getting to Grips with Anxiety: A Guided Self-Help Workbook* by Barker *et al.* (2021) and supplementary manuals for working with panic, worry, phobias and other conditions; and *Behavioural Activation for Young People with Low Mood: A Guided Self-Help Manual* (2021) by Zoe Maiden. Many thanks to Kings College London, South London and Maudesley NHS Trust and the Anna Freud Centre for making these freely available.

ADVANCED INTERVENTIONS

For a helpful overview of assessment, formulation and intervention, try *CBT with Children, Young People and Families* (2017) by Peter Fuggle, Sandra Dunsmuir and Vicki Curry.

For more specific intervention guidance as used by high intensity CBT therapists, try:

Breaking Free from OCD (2008) by Jo Derisley, Isabel Heyman, Sarah Robinson and Cynthia Turner.

PTSD: CBT with Children and Young People (2010) by Patrick Smith, Sean Perrin, William Yule and David M. Clark.

Depression: Cognitive Behaviour Therapy with Children and Young People by Chrissie Verduyn, Julia Rogers and Alison Wood.

GOAL-BASED OUTCOMES

www.goals-in-therapy.com is a great resource explaining GBOs and how to use them.

WORKING WITH IDENTITY AND DIFFERENCE

The 'IAPT Black, Asian and Minority Ethnic Service User Positive Practice Guide' is available for free at www.babcp.com. Dr Brendan J Dunlop's *The Queer Mental Health Workbook* (2022) is a useful resource for those working with older LGBTQ+ identifying teenagers.

THERAPEUTIC CONVERSATIONS

The 'Positive Practice Guide for Working with Children and Young People' issued by BABCP has some good tips – also from www.babcp.com

A fantastic guide on 'doing' Socratic dialogue is 'Socratic questions with children: Recommendations and cautionary tales' by McLachlan, Eastwood and Friedberg (2016).

Another is the small *Socratic Method* booklet by Helen Kennerley (2007).

HELPING WITH SELF-HARM

Cutting Down: A CBT Workbook for Treating Young People Who Self-Harm (Schmitt, Simic and Taylor, 2015) is a great resource.

COMPASSION-FOCUSED APPROACHES

The Kindness Workbook: Creative and Compassionate Ways to Boost Your Wellbeing has lots of great ideas – by Elaine Beaumont and Mary Welford (2020).

Three great websites are:

www.compassionatemind.co.uk

https://self-compassion.org

http://chrisgermer.com

SLEEP

Why We Sleep by Mike Walker (2018) is a fascinating read.

www.enlightenyourclock.org hosts a great psychoeducation booklet explaining the science of sleep to teenagers.

A sleep checklist can be found in the resources at: www.mentally-healthyschools.org.uk

'Healthy sleep tips for children' is available at www.nhs.uk/live-well/sleep-and-tiredness/healthy-sleep-tips-for-children

OTHER

For more on motivational interviewing, read *A Clinician's Guide to Think Good-Feel Good: Using CBT with Children and Young People* by Paul Stallard (2005).

For more on PTSD and trauma: www.uktraumacouncil.org

For lots on whole school wellbeing approaches, resources in schools and much more: www.mentallyhealthyschools.org.uk

Lots of EMHPs recommend *The Mentally Healthy Schools Workbook* (2020) by Pooky Knightsmith, as well as Andrew Cowley's *The Wellbeing Toolkit* (2019).

Nicola Morgan's *Blame My Brain: The Amazing Teenage Brain Revealed* (2013) does exactly what it says on the cover.

About the Author

Hugh is a postgraduate clinical tutor at the Anna Freud Centre and an honorary lecturer at University College London. He has helped teach, train and supervise children's wellbeing practitioners, education mental health practitioners and supervisors on the children and young people IAPT programmes. Originally qualifying as a child psychotherapist, Hugh worked for over ten years as a practitioner embedded in schools – including in a pilot mental health support team project. Alongside his teaching work, Hugh continues to work as a cognitive behavioural psychotherapist and supervisor within Specialist CAMHS.

Index